Murphy's Law with a Side of Serendipity

By

Dana Frye

Dedication

I dedicate this book to my family and friends,
whose love and presence have been my strength
in both joy and challenge.

Always grateful,
Dana Frye

Contents

Prologue

Help me, Oh Please Help me! I must be having a heart attack; I can't breathe! My heart is racing, and every breath I take is racked with excruciating pain. I feel like I'm about to die. I want to call for my husband, but the pain has taken away my ability to scream. I lay on the sofa praying my husband will be done showering before I expire. Finally, I heard my husband ask me, "Are you ok"? I try to sit up, but to no avail. I tell him to take me to the hospital. He helps me stand, but I cannot stand straight; I walk slowly to our van, bent over like an overcooked green bean. As my husband drives me to the hospital, I am lying in the back seat, curled up in a fetal position, praying I make it. "Dear God, let me live." As they put my aching body on a gurney, all I can do is cry. I am wheeled into the emergency room, and every bump feels like a cannonball is bouncing in my chest. I take shallow breaths to avoid the knife-stabbing pain that is ripping my body apart! I am hooked up to a heart monitor and IV for fluids in one arm as well as a blood pressure cuff on the other. A thermometer in my mouth and a nurse asking me questions.

All I keep saying is, please stop the pain! Please give me something to stop the pain!!! The doctor will be right in, and we will get you something for the pain. What feels like a lifetime later, a doctor enters my room and starts asking me questions that I cannot answer. My husband is trying his best to answer the doctor's questions, and again, I'm mumbling for pain medication. The Doctor orders a chest x-ray and tells me he will be back in a little bit. I am beginning to feel overcome by the pain and crying out in pain when the technician comes in to do a chest x-ray. "I need you to lay on your back so we can do a chest x-ray."

As they raise the bed upright, I am in so much pain the tears are rolling down my cheeks like a leak in a garden hose. Fifteen minutes later, I heard the Doctor telling my husband, "Her right lung is 45% collapsed, and we need to insert a chest tube." I once again plead for pain medication. The Doctor explains they have to install a chest tube, and I need to be alert and awake for the procedure to be successful. He assures me that he will give me pain medication as soon as the chest tube is inserted. I am asking why did this happen? He tells me it is called a spontaneous pneumothorax, which sometimes happens without trauma or injury to people who are thin-built like yourself.

Within five minutes, a medical team of 5 was in my room telling me I had to lie on my left side so they could do the procedure. "I can't. I will die"! It took 5 pillows and a blanket to prop me on my left side. I am shivering and cold while they soak my entire right side with an antibacterial spray. As a nurse holds up my right arm, I am told I will feel a small pinch from the needle giving me novocaine. Then without warning, the Doctor cuts a 1" slit in my side. I scream out in pain! Next, the Dr takes a 1" hard rigid plastic tube and shoves it in the hole through my rib cage and tells me to take a deep breath. I can tell you if there was ever a time I wanted to die, it is now!

Mary

Mary tries to keep walking but the pain has derailed her to a bench on Haddon Ave. She brushes off a light covering of snow from earlier that day to sit down. Only 3 more blocks to go, and this will be over. As she takes a deep breath, she picks up her overnight bag and continues her journey. It's bitterly cold and dark; she wishes she would have taken the time to put her boots on instead of slipping on her penny loafers. The sidewalks were icy, and as she reached her destination, she was shivering from the night air. She now wonders how she will ever tackle a dozen steps to reach the front door of Lady of Lourdes Hospital.

With Deep breaths and minor rest stops, she finally makes it to the revolving doors of the entrance, and she summons for help as she crouches over from pain. As a nurse puts Mary in a wheelchair, she is frazzled, cold, and in severe pain and is asking for pain medication. She just walked 5 blocks on a cold Fridget night in active labor.

As they wheel Mary to the 4th floor, she prays for the moment that this will all be over and she can return to the life she knew, with her fifteen-month-old daughter awaiting her return. She had already completed all the necessary paperwork, and now all she had left to do was deliver this baby she carried.

Early the next morning, on December 17, 1959, Mary is awakened by the nurse who is asking her how she feels. Mary asks, "Is my baby ok"? "What did I have"? Your baby girl is beautiful. Would you like to see her? Mary replies, "Yes, and I would like to have her christened before I leave." So, as Mary requested, a Catholic priest was brought into her hospital room, and Mary christened her baby girl, "Teresa Ann" named after Saint Teresa, the patron saint "Little Flower" Teresa Ann who would never know her, who she held only once in her arms, would be whisked away 10 minutes after she was christened. Mary knew nothing about where her baby girl Teresa Ann was going but believed wherever she went would be better than what she could offer her.

Two days later, Mary would be gone, discharged from the hospital, and back to continue her life with her husband and her 15-month-old daughter.

John

John was raised in South Philadelphia in an area that was called "The Village." John was the third son born to James and Agnes, who immigrated and came over on a ship. James from Ireland, and Agnes from the Ukraine. They met, married, and built their home in which their four boys and one daughter were raised. In the 1920s, indoor plumbing was only for the rich or unheard of, so John, as well as his four siblings, were accustomed to growing up with an outhouse. John was raised by a father who worked as an elevator operator for the railroad and made very little money. Although John grew up in a family that was considered poor, he grew up knowing he and his siblings were very much loved.

As a young boy, John used to bring the family pony into Philadelphia, offering pony rides for a nickel each. It was then John would be known as Yankie, from "Yankie Doodle Dandy." In his teenage years, John would pick on the dump and sell what he found with worth. He would use these pennies, nickels, and dimes to go to the movie theater on Saturday with his buddies. The movie theater is where he meets his true love and forever soul mate, Joanie.

While they were being typical teenage boys and throwing popcorn across the theater, he hit the head of the lady who would become his bride. According to Johnny, he hit the jackpot!

Joanie

Joanie was raised in a South Philadelphia neighborhood considered to be middle to upper class in the early 1930s; Joanie would be the 6th child of 7 born to Joseph and Marie. Joseph, who so loved Marie and proposed to marry, went to the extreme of changing his Italian name to an Irish one in order to marry Marie.

Back in the early 1900s, it was considered taboo to marry a different nationality, race, or religion. Therefore, by changing the last letter of his last name, he could legally marry the Irish Catholic Marie without objections from her family.

Joanie attended St. Monica's Catholic School in her elementary years and then completed her High School career at John W Hallahan, an all-girls high school. Joanie and her best friend Sue often would go shopping together downtown where they would have to take a public bus, as very few families had cars in the city.

It was on a Saturday afternoon they decided to go to the picture show downtown where Joanie would meet John because she was hit in the head with a popcorn kernel. Annoyed at the immaturity of John and his buddies throwing popcorn, she still agreed to meet John the following Saturday at the theater for their first real date.

The following week, when Joanie arrived at the theater, she did not see John- so feeling impatient, she paid for her ticket and entered the theater. When John showed up a few minutes later, and sat down next to her and apologized for being late. Joanie looked at John and said, as she held out her hand, "No problem, just give me the movie fare back."

At the mere age of 15, Joanie knew John was the one, so when John went into the service a year after they began dating, she vowed to wait for him.

Engaged

Till Death Do Us Part is what John and Joanie decided in 1953. John proposed to Joanie, and Joanie accepted but told John the diamond was too small. John replaced it with a beautiful platinum band with a 1/2 karat round center diamond and smaller diamonds on each side. Joanie and John will now plan their wedding, which will take place on September 11, 1954. They were married in St Monica's Catholic Church in South Philadelphia.

Joanie wore a beautiful white wedding dress adorned in lace and pearls, equipped with a very long train and a traditional veil. They celebrated a reception at Marka John Hall on Broad St in Philadelphia. After the beautiful wedding, they had a honeymoon in Atlantic City, NJ. They did not move into an apartment as most couples did in 1954 but rather bought a brand-new house in Delsea Estates in Clayton, NJ. They both worked in Philadelphia, Joanie for a lawyer and John for Union Tank. They would drive their old Plymouth with no heat to Philadelphia and freeze their butts off going to work each day.

Pancakes were dinner at least 3 times a week, but they wanted to save to start a family. They wanted to have children; they wanted the white picket fence, with a backyard for their children to play and fresh Jersey air to breathe. Two years later, they sold the Little House in Clayton, NJ, and purchased a Cape Cod in Colonial Manor in Woodbury, NJ. After no babies in four years, Joanie was diagnosed with endometriosis and told her chances of conceiving were zero.

Rather than giving up their dream of having a family, they applied to Catholic Charities to adopt. In March of 1960, they brought home a baby girl whom they named "Dana Marie"

My Arrival

I'd be lying if I told you I remembered coming home or that I remembered anything about the house to which I came home. I am told that by my second birthday, my parents sold the Cape Cod house in Woodbury and built a brand new 2-story colonial in Sewell, NJ. This was the home where my earliest memories began. I can recall screaming in my crib until my mother would come in and bring me into her bed to sleep on her stomach. I recall being a very fearful child. I think I was afraid of everything! I recall green heads in the windows of my bedroom which would keep me up crying. I recall being afraid of a blind man who played the accordion in Southwood Shopping Center, where my mother often shopped.

I used to dislike the dark and would sleep with the light on every night. However, one of my biggest fears was going to kindergarten. I did not want to go, and I cried every morning when my mother would drop me off. I was one of those children that daycare centers hate! I was a child who was also born with many allergies. I recall many trips to Children's Hospital in Philadelphia for allergy shots. I was allergic to dust, mold, mildew, ragweed, milk, chocolate, eggs, and the list went on.

When I was only 5 years old, I was told to pack my Barbie suitcase to go with my mother to visit my grandmother in Philadelphia. However, I was not going to see my grandmother; instead, I was going to Underwood Hospital and being admitted to have my tonsils and adenoids removed! I will never forget screaming my head off when my mother left me there! It was one of those childhood traumas you never forget.

One of the happiest memories I recall was at age four when my parents brought home my baby sister. She was so tiny, and I would just sit and watch her sleep in her bassinet, feeling so much pride and joy that I was now the big sister.

Childhood Antics

My first friend was Kim, who lived across the street, and I was not permitted to cross. The street I grew up on was a dead-end street with 9 houses on it, but still, my mother insisted on walking me across the street.

When I was about six years old, my father bought a 20 ft Cobia Cabin Cruiser in which the family would go down to Money Island, Gandy's Beach, or Fortescue, where we would take the boat out on the bay for fishing excursions. I absolutely loved the boat, and my Dad taught me to fish, and bait my own rod.

I can recall catching flounder, weakfish, bluefish, oyster crackers, and blowfish. It was always amazing for me. However, my mother and sister would suffer from being seasick and would spend most of the day in the cabin.

Eventually, it became just Dad and I going on these fishing trips; it was our special times. I was about 9 when my father bought a 26ft Grady White Cabin Cruiser, which had a built-in fish box on the floor, and we would pack it with fish to bring home. This was our special time that I will never forget. When I was in the 2nd grade, I made friends with a girl who lived in the woods adjacent to Tall Pines Golf Course right in front of the green.

At the end of my street, there was a dirt path that was a big downward hill that would lead to her house. She and I would become best friends and enjoy so many great times that our memories are both cherished and unforgettable. We were child entrepreneurs to start. We would make cool aid and sell it on the street for a nickel a glass. We would weed neighbors' gardens and get paid to play with a French poodle named Suzie. But our biggest windfall would come from walking on the golf course and collecting golf balls in the woods and the creek, which we would clean and shine in the golf ball washer located on the golf course.

We would place them in individual bags and then sell them to the casual golfers who may have lost their balls. We would then get on our bicycles and ride to the Gurk's Store.

Back in 1966-67, Gurk's was a store that basically sold bread and milk, a limited amount of can goods, and household items. Gurk's had an old-fashioned soda machine filled with all kinds of bottled soda, and my favorite was cream soda. But the reason for our 5-block bike ride was for the biggest candy counter we had ever seen! Every kind of candy made was at Gurk's. We bought the bright color dot candy affixed to a white paper strip, redfish, wax lips filled with sweet juice, Maryjane candies, chocolate cups filled with peanut butter, and round saucer candy filled with hard pellets, but our biggest purchase would be the bazooka, bubble gum wrapped with a comic and horoscope strip inside.

We would leave Gurk's with so much bubble gum in our mouths that we would look like hamsters. It's the days of the '60s when we went outside to play right after breakfast and wouldn't come home till dinner time, then back out again until the street lights came on. We would climb trees, build forts in the woods, play red light, green light, red rover, hopscotch, and hide and seek.

We would go sledding when it snowed on Tall Pines Golf Course, which was filled with huge hills! We would roller skate on the sidewalks with the roller skates that would go on under your shoes and never have breaks! I would come home filthy, sometimes with bumps and bruises and abrasions on my knees that may have needed a squirt of Bactine and a band-aid, but thankfully, never a broken bone.

The craziest thing we did in the 60s was chasing the mosquito truck on our bikes; we would be riding in a cloud of toxic chemicals. This, of course, was before environmental testing and knowledge.

In 1969, I got the worst news of my childhood when my grandmother passed away. It was the first time I ever saw my father cry, and it was my first experience of fatality. In 1971, my heart was broken for the second time when my parents sold our house and told me we were moving to a house on Sherwin Rd in Richwood, NJ. This was a farm area famous for growing peaches and apples. I was going to have to change schools and leave my best friend. This was bad news for me.

My sister was only in 1st grade, but I had just finished the 5th grade and only had one more year left to finish elementary school. I wanted no part of this move! The real complication occurred when we had to move into a motel room in West Deptford, NJ because the house my parents were having built was not finished. Imagine 2 adults and 2 children living in a motel room. Everything we owned except clothing went into storage! My father was a truck driver and was gone most of the week; he would leave at 4 am and sometimes not get home until 9 or 10 pm. My mother had to drive us to the new school that I hated and pick us up in the afternoon.

We ate dinner just about every night at the Green Tree Restaurant. It was very boring for 11 weeks living this way. The best memory of Maple Motel was when I became friends with the owner's daughter, Rosie. This motel sat on 295 and Grove Rd., and many truckers would stay at this motel for rest. The worst memory of this motel and really my entire childhood, was when Rosie had the idea that we climb on a truck to reach the roof of the motel.

Well, I received the worst beating of my life when Rosie's father told my Dad we were running on the roof! Back in the 1970's, the belt was most commonly a father's form of discipline, and it was not frowned upon; imagine that! We finally moved into our new L- shaped 2000 square foot rancher, but I will never forget the Maple Motel!

New House

By the end of October 1971, we finally moved into the new house. My sister and I had our own bathroom with brass mirrors that hung over our sinks, we had our own bedrooms, and the house was so much bigger than our old one. This house was my parent's fourth home, and every one of them was brand new, but this house was custom-built and was the cream of the crop. I recall that four months after we moved in, a brand-new patio and built-in swimming pool were installed.

My father was very handy and built brick walkways and steps down to the pool from the patio. It was an outdoor oasis. The interior of the home was filled with fine furniture and decor. My mother was a self-taught seamstress and made beautiful gold velvet slipcovers and matching drapes in the living room. It look-ed like a home you would see in a Better Homes and Gardens magazine.

It took me a month or better to get on board with the move but after making a friend who would become my first crush who lived across the street, things began to become better. His name was Jeff, and we became a couple, secretively stealing kisses on our walks in the woods behind my house. There was a huge oak tree in the front corner of my front yard, which was in line with Jeff's driveway. This tree had a hole in the bark about 3 feet high, just large enough for Jeff and I to place love notes to one another. It became our secret mailbox. We had that perfect puppy love that my heart will always remember. I also made friends with Annie and Donna, who were in my class at school.

Times were getting better. Annie and I had some good times; her mother acted as our personal chauffeur and would drive us anywhere we wanted to go. We would visit with her neighbor, an elderly man in his late 60s or early 70s, around the corner from her house; he would buy us juice boxes and candy to have snacks ready when we visited. He lived alone, and when I look back on it today, I realize that he probably was a person we never should have been visiting. He told us to call him Uncle Harry. I can't say for sure, but this Uncle Harry may have been dangerous! Lucky for us, we never found out.

What I recall the most about 6th grade is a project we had to do on family genetics; we had to bring in a picture of the person we looked most like. Well, I did not look like either of my parents, naturally, since they were not biologically related. I knew from about the age of four when they adopted my sister. This was when my mother told me that I was the chosen one. She told me that God chose me for them. So, as a child, I always knew I was adopted.

However, it was now presenting me with a problem. My father said his sister, My Aunt Sissy, who was my favorite aunt, looked similar to me at my age. So, when Aunt Sis gave me the photo of her when she was 12- I almost fell on the floor! The resemblance was striking! Same facial features and blonde hair- it was the solution to not only my 6th-grade project but now I believed I had found my biological mother. You know about all those family secrets you hear about on Oprah Winfrey, well at the age of 12, I was convinced that my Aunt Sissy, who never married, somehow got pregnant and gave me to my parents.

Certainly, it made sense to me; she always did so much for me that all the other nieces and nephews missed out on. She bought me a white fur coat with a matching muff and beautiful dresses from Bamburgers and John Wanamakers. She was my God Mother and we would go Christmas Shopping together. She was the nicest aunt, and now I knew why. Although my parents denied it, I continued believing she was my biological mother. As time moved on, I accepted the move and the new house, but I knew that next year, I would see all my old friends when I entered Clearview Junior High because Clearview was a regional Junior and Senior High School. It encompassed students from both Mantua and Harrison Townships. My old house was in Mantua, Twp., and the new one was in Harrison, Twp. So, in a short time, I would see my old friends again.

Junior High Curse

My school clothes and supplies were ready, and my excitement was growing as it was very close to starting at my new school. Junior High!

I couldn't have been happier. I was going to see my old friends again! However, that excitement soon turned to anxiety when, the day before school would start, I would be confronted with womanhood. Why did my menstrual cycle have to come now? It was going to ruin my first day! The cramps were fierce, and having to wear a sanitary napkin, which in 1973 was a size fitted for an elephant, was just not fair! I guess the day was not what I expected, but I carefully got through it with many halls passes to navigate to the lady's room.

I recall changing classrooms with 7 different teachers and a study hall, but the best thing about junior high was the huge cafeteria rocking "Hold Your Head Up" by a band called Argent, blaring loudly every day at lunch. The sad part was my best friend Sue was not in any of my classes, we didn't even have the same lunch. However, it didn't matter because after only attending junior high for one month, it was all over. You see, there was a group of very mean girls who started antagonizing me on the bus ride to and from school. They did not like me, and for what reason, I would never know. It was at the beginning of October when these girls got off my bus stop and followed behind me. This one short little bitch started shoving me and egging me to fight. I tried to walk away, but after she grabbed me by my hair, I decided that would be the last time she would do that. I recall that I kept punching her in her face until there was blood on my knuckles. This marked my first catfight and the last time I would attend junior high. My mother, of course, was called by the bus driver and the principal from school, and even though I was not the instigator, my mother was not allowing me to attend a school where violence was tolerated. The very next day, my mother took me to Saint Joseph's Catholic School in Swedesboro, NJ, where she enrolled me, and I would begin the following Monday. I had to wear a uniform that consisted of a blue plaid skirt and a round-collared white blouse.

This would be my fourth school and once again, making me the new kid in school! St. Joe's was a small school with no changing classes and no jukebox in the cafeteria; in fact, the cafeteria was in the basement. The only good thing was I again had a recess after lunch. The playground was a fenced-in parking lot with no swings or equipment, just a blacktop. We had to use our imagination and find ways to amuse ourselves. I will never forget running into a metal pole that was part of the cyclone fencing and breaking my front tooth. My mother had to pick me up from school and take me to the dentist, where I had to have root canal work and a cap put on my left top front tooth! Of course, my mother cried; she said I had perfect teeth, and now I didn't.

My classmates consisted of 11 girls and 18 boys. It was a very quaint school even for the 1970's. The big difference was having an extra class mandatory to take, Religion Class; I had taken CCD classes through my church as a child and made all my sacraments. However, since we attended Catholic school, daily religion classes and morning prayers over the intercom were mandatory. I also recall all the girls would walk to St Joseph's Church, a block away from the school, to sing for funeral services. I adjusted well, made friends, and made many wonderful memories for 7th grade. I must say that although I did not want to come to St Joe's, it awarded me one of my best lifetime friends. Jane and I cherish all the firsts we experienced together. Especially sneaking 7&7's at her uncle's birthday party. It was fun going down but horrible coming up! That was the day I vowed never to drink alcoholic beverages again! We spent summers down Sea Aisle City, NJ, babysitting. Jane for her brother and sisters and me for two boys I babysat at home, who were friends with her parents. The funniest memory I have of Jane is the day we were swimming in the ocean, and a wave pulled me under and took my bikini bottom with it! I had to walk back to our beach house wrapped in a towel with nothing under it! It's funny now, but at the time, I was devastated. Eighth grade also had wonderful memories, and upon graduation, our class consisted of nine girls and 14 boys. We wore blue graduation gowns and caps and were excited about entering High School. I would be attending St James HS in Carney's Point, NJ. My freshman year.

High School Days

St James High School had a very long bus ride. I would get on the bus at 6:15 am and get to school at 8:30 am. It was grueling, to say the least. It was on this bus ride I would meet Denise who would become another best friend. We had a couple of hours every day to get to know each other, and she became one of my favorites. During this long ride, our bus driver, Si, who was very cool, would play an 8-track tape every day. He was trying to make the ride more enjoyable. Every day, I would ride on the bus listening to "Truckin" by Grateful Dead," this song would be repeated at least 5 times each ride. I often wondered why a bus filled with Catholic HS students would find joy in the Grateful Dead. But the bigger question I had was why a Catholic HS would have a smoking area outside in which students were allowed to partake. This would be why I took up smoking. It was cool, and I had to be part of the cool group. Probably the biggest mistake of my life!

I was also turned off by a math teacher who was touching the girl's legs under the table, myself included. St James classes were set up with 20-minute mods. The class would consist of 6-8 students sitting at a round table with the teacher in the middle. It was determined that small groups could accomplish as much learning in 20 minutes as large classes could in 40. So, since all the classes were only 20-minute mods, it left time for more classes or, in most cases, more free time to do nothing. I did not like this HS at all! I would spend hours begging my mother to go back to Clearview High School. It was the summer after freshman year I finally convinced her to allow me to register in Clearview for my sophomore year. I still kept in touch with Jane and a few other girls who stayed at St. James and Denise, who also left St. James to attend West Deptford HS., but the day I walked back through the doors of Clearview HS was one of my happiest moments.

I auditioned for cheerleading and made the squad, probably one of my biggest accomplishments. The pride I felt was indescribable when I saw my name amongst the 12, hanging on a poster in front of the gym; I made the team! It was in my sophomore year I met my first Real love. He was a star on the basketball team, and I was a cheerleader; we spent half our sophomore year and half of our junior year together. He was 6ft 6," and I stood 5ft 5." We attended dances at the HS, where we cringed when the song "Hold Me Kiss Me Thrill Me" was played because it was always the last song of the night! We were the perfect couple until we weren't. I fell hard, and when he told me he wanted to date others, it crushed me beyond words! I actually suffered from a broken heart, couldn't eat, and felt lost. I can remember having lumps in my throat where I actually felt sick to my stomach! This went on until I found a new beau.

The new guy was probably not a good idea, but rebounds never are. The relationship with Jerry did not last long, however we did have some good times. My mother made us Halloween costumes that won 1st prize, at High School. We dressed up as Jolly Green Giant and Little Sprout. We painted our faces, arms, and shoulders green! My mother was one fantastic seamstress! I believe we won "Most Original." However, we were complete opposites though, and the relationship would be cut short after we had a bad car accident together. A friend of Jerry's who had one too many beers crashed us into a telephone pole! I can recall seeing despair on my father's face upon carrying me on a stretcher from the ambulance into the hospital. I was forbidden to see Jerry again!

18th Birthday

It was December of 1977, on my 18th birthday, my parents bought me my 1st car. She was a beauty! 1972 Mercury Comet GT! Gold with black racing stripes, she had a ram air induction on the hood and an engine that kicked ass! 302cid V8. The only problem now was I had to get a job to pay to insure her! In January of 1978, I began working as a waitress at 76 Truck Stop in Paulsboro, NJ. It was a busy place filled with truckers; however, being raised by a truck driver, I had no qualms. I would go to work Friday, Saturday, Sunday, and Monday from 3-11. I didn't make a killing, but I made enough to insure my car and put gas in it. Life was good, but freedom was still stifled. I had rules and curfews that needed to be met, or the keys would be withheld, to my regret. Growing up in the 60's and 70's had a common rule that my generation was familiar with (as long as you live under my roof, you will follow my rules). End of story!

It was in my senior year I met the man I would marry. It was in March of 1978 when I went to a pub called Mazzeo's Cafe in Glassboro, NJ, and I noticed him right away. He was tall and handsome, and we began talking. By the end of the night, we exchanged phone numbers. When my HS graduation was celebrated, we were going steady. We also set up 3 of my friends with 3 of his friends. The 8 of us would travel together: Pocono Mountains trip, Wildwood, camping, and Trips to the local pubs. We really had great times. We used to play card games and Michigan Rummy. Drink beer in the street and have Jack in the Box runs for midnight snacks but in my case, 11:30 snacks.

In the grand scheme of things, life was good! The only thing that presented a problem these days would be my curfew being midnight. If I wasn't home by midnight, I'd be grounded.

Wedding times

Christmas in 1978, my boyfriend Gary bought me a hope chest. Now, in those days, a hope chest meant marriage. It was purchased to pack with mementos in the hope that marriage was the next step. My girlfriend Debbie and I began working in a factory called "Winter Chemicals." This company produced oil and brake fluid, transmission fluid, and all kinds of chemicals for cars. It was a dirty and boring job. We would sit on stools and put caps on bottles as they whizzed by on the assembly line, sometimes faster than our fingers could keep up with. We were Laverne and Shirley to a fault! Our Line Leader was a guy named John, who I became fast friends with. He and I would become very close; we shared December birthdays, he on the 16th and mine on the 17th. We would be true Comrades forever! I recall buying lunch from the Lunch Truck outside the factory and Debbie and I eating lunch in one of our cars. Since we carpooled each morning, we often would be talking about how we could get out of work and just drive to Wildwood for the day and bask in the sun.

We had great hours, Monday through Friday, 7 AM- 3:30 PM, no weekends, and home for dinner. Even though, the hours were good, we were still awaiting the day we got married and had children. We really both hated living at home with our parents and all the rules that went with it.

Debbie was dating one of Gary's friends, John, who was one of the 4 couples; we played matchmaker. Both Debbie and I were vying for engagement rings. In the late 70's it was common to be married before 21. Girls were raised to believe marriage and children were the only expectations we needed to achieve. There were some girls we graduated with that went on to college, but the majority got jobs and dreamed of being married with children. I do not recall the day, but it was an ordinary night in which Gary proposed and it was in his car in front of my house. I believe it was cold outside, and sometime before Thanksgiving.

Debbie received her diamond around the same time. It became a race to the church to pick our wedding date. We wanted September, but no date in September was available. We picked August 30, 1980. Debbie and John married on October 4, 1980. Although we were close friends, we were not bridesmaids at each other's weddings due to the close proximity of our weddings.

In the end, I believe an argument occurred because we had the same friends on both sides; the bride and groom's friends could not afford to be in two weddings! I picked my best friend, Denise, to be my Maid of Honor and 5 bridesmaids. My sister Kelly, my sister-in-law Kim, and Jane, who was my long-time friend from St Joe's.

Debbie—a different Debbie—dated Frank, who is another friend of Gary's. Janet dated Paul, who was also Gary's friend. All the girls looked beautiful in Southern style, off-the-shoulder, pink chiffon gowns. I wanted to wear my mother's wedding dress, but it was too small. I found a traditional lace and pearl gown at a Bridal shop called "Seventh Heaven." My gown was beautiful, to say the least. My mother made my veil that looked almost exactly like what Princess Diana wore when she married Prince Charles. Everything was all I dreamed it would be.

We attended pre-marital classes at Incarnation Church, which was a must to be married in the Catholic Church. What I remember that stands out most in my mind during my engagement was my mother asking me what I was using for birth control. It surprised me, but I think I surprised her more when I said nothing because we were not having sex! We were waiting until we were married. My mother didn't believe me at first, I mean all those weekend trips together and you have done nothing? It took me for a loop! My mother told me that something was not right, and I better find out before I married. She found it odd that a young man made no attempt with those raging hormones.

Everything was going as planned until about 5 weeks before the wedding, and I began feeling sick. I was vomiting to the point where nothing was staying down. It took every ounce of energy I had to get up out of bed! Everything smelled funny, and just a faint scent of tomato sauce would send me heaving! My girlfriend Denise said could you be pregnant? Oh no! We went to the drug store and purchased a pregnancy test, and when that little blue line showed up positive, it was the first time in my life I wished I never took my mother's advice! My wedding was 4 1/2 weeks away and I would be with child! I cried but tried to remain steadfast to the fact that it's only 4 1/2 weeks, and we'll get through this.

On August 30, 1980, at 3:00 pm, I was married in Incarnation Church. Everything was so beautiful. We hired a professional photographer who took beautiful pictures to capture the most amazing memories of my wedding. Our reception was held at a Catering Hall in Bridgeton, NJ. Gia's Suburban House. It was a distance to travel and pay 5 limousines to drive us, but it was the most beautiful reception hall that was adorned with white lights, a fountain with a waterfall, and a lifted bridal table that sat 4 feet off the floor.

The food was delicious, and the DJ was fabulous. It was your traditional wedding reception where I danced with my father to "Daddy's Little Girl," and the happy couple did all the hoopla, such as removing the garter, throwing the bouquet, making rounds to all the tables of our 175 guests, collecting envelopes that were placed in my white satin money bag that my mother made me. The day would have been perfect if only I wasn't sick! We left the next day to go on our honeymoon in the Pocono Mountains. It was a Honeymoon Resort in which our room had a heart shaped jacuzzi and mirrors everywhere!

We played games in the nightclub at night, such as the Newlywed Game and a game called Pick Your Groom. The men would roll up their pant legs, and they blindfolded the women, and we were expected to pick out our husbands by feeling their legs! We saw music bands, went horseback riding, and played pool and pinball in the game room. Wonderful meals were included, but I barely got a morsel down. We did everything but what was expected on a honeymoon. You might say.... It was a Honeymoon from Hell!

New House and a Baby

After we returned from our honeymoon, I set up an appointment with an obstetrician to find out about the pregnancy and hoped that they could give me something for the nausea and vomiting. I had an appointment with a group of doctors at JFK Hospital in Stratford, NJ. During my first visit, I discovered that I was suffering from hyperemesis gravidarum, a condition that affects some pregnant women. It was new back in the 80s, but it is the same condition Princess Kate suffered with during her multiple pregnancies. However, my condition was so severe I was hospitalized at 6 months of my pregnancy because I had lost 20 lbs instead of gaining weight.

I recall saying to my husband that this is the first and last baby you will ever have by me. It was so bad they put me on a drug, Bendectin, which was later determined to cause major birth defects; I was shaking in my shoes that my child would be damaged with missing limbs. This is the information:

So, this is what I had to live with during the last trimester of my pregnancy. Being my first pregnancy, I had enough fear brewing over the delivery, and now I was absolutely frightened that my baby could have devastating effects from the Bendectin that I was prescribed. Back in 1981, ultrasounds were not routine testing; therefore, I had no idea of my baby's sex or if the baby was healthy. I was given a due date of April 1st, and during my obstetrician visits, the doctor was guessing I was having a boy.

By February, my nausea and vomiting subsided to allow me to eat some bland foods, but still, No spaghetti, pizza, or tomato sauce, as the slightest scent did me in. My husband had taken a job as a craps dealer in Atlantic City, NJ, working long hours, and he was rarely home. We rented a 1-bedroom apartment in Pine Hill, NJ, but we spent very little time there. I spent all my days at my parent's home, where my mother and I would make frequent trips to Friendly's Ice Cream parlor . We would order Big Hot Fudge Sundaes. I started to pack on the pounds by the last month.

I can still recall on April 1st driving to my parent's house and feeling cramping. By 3 PM that afternoon, I knew I was in labor! My first thought was, wow!!! I'm going to have this baby on my due date. By 5 PM, the contractions were 5 minutes apart, so I called my husband at work to let him know I was going to the hospital. My mother drove me, and my girlfriend Denise met me at the hospital.

Upon an examination, I was told I was only 1 centimeter dilated, and it would be a while; a baby is not born until a woman reaches 10 centimeters. All I could think was, OMG!!!!! I am not going to have my baby tonight. When my husband Gary arrived, both my mother and Denise left. I believe it was around 9 PM when he finally arrived at the hospital.

By midnight, the contractions were getting stronger, and all the natural childbirth classes Gary and I took weren't helping at all! I had my pretty focal point on the wall and was trying my hardest to focus on the breathing exercises—breathing and panting when the contractions hit—but nothing could have prepared me for that intense pain. By morning, I was telling the nurse I wanted an epidural. However, Dr. Steinberg, who I will refer to as Dr. Iceberg, said I was only 3 centimeters, and I needed to wait until I was further along.

By noon on April 2nd, I was exhausted and dehydrated and had to have an IV for fluids. Gary was falling asleep in the chair, and I was becoming an irritated bitch! My mother came back to the hospital around 5 PM so Gary could get a break to eat and recharge. The nurse allowed both Gary and my mother to stay in the room. By 7 P.m., the doctor added Pitocin to my IV. Pitocin is a drug used to speed up labor. Again, I asked for an epidural and was told that if I got an epidural, it would slow down the process and prevent the Pitocin from working. However, what Dr Iceberg failed to tell me was that the labor pains were going to become fast and furious. It was the worst pain I ever experienced, and I was becoming delirious from the pain!

At 10 PM, Dr Iceberg came in with a long metal hook that looked like a knitting needle and broke my water. The next 4 hours were pure Hell! I was falling asleep in between contractions that were coming every 45 seconds. My mother had taken over as my coach while Gary slept soundly, snoring in the chair. I remember her arguing with the nurses, demanding something to help with the pain, but by then, it was too late!

Finally, at 2:30 AM, the nurse was wheeling me down to the delivery room. Gary was awake and putting on paper sanitary scrubs to enter the Delivery Room. I was put on a cold metal table, and I remember the room was freezing, and I was shivering. As they told me to push, I felt like I was ripping apart! I must have pushed for quite a while, and at **3:04 AM on 4/3/1981**, after 34 hours of labor, I delivered my beautiful baby girl, Kristin. She was 8 lbs and 5 ozs. 21" long with a 9 as her Apgar score. She had dark black hair and blue eyes and was healthy. I was truly blessed and the happiest girl in the world.

Back in 1981, they kept mothers and babies for 3 days in the hospital. The babies did not stay in the mother's room but in a baby's nursery. Because I was breastfeeding, they were bringing Kristin to my room every 3 hours around the clock. I had a roommate who also had a baby girl, and she and I would end up friends by discharge. After all, we had daughters born on the same day.

After being discharged, It was decided we would stay at my parents' house so I would have help with the baby.; Gary would be going back to work, and I didn't want to be alone. Sleep deprived from nursing and nipples that were actually bleeding from my hungry baby girl. Kristin also had colic and barely slept long enough for me to catch a wink. It was a trying time, but to make matters worse, our dog, Monique, was hit by a car and killed on the day we came home! It was not an easy time. Gary and I were sleeping in my old bedroom in a twin bed. Not that it mattered much because I was up nights with Kristin, walking her in my arms while she cried in pain from the Colic.

After 3 months with my parents, we purchased a small rancher in Clayton, NJ. We decorated Kristin's room with a Strawberry Shortcake theme, and my father came over and helped paint the kitchen cabinets and install a new floor in the kitchen. It wasn't a Palace, but it was home! In September of 1981, my best friend Denise married, and I was her Maid of Honor. Her wedding was in South Philadelphia and I recall it was the most fun I had since Kristin was born.

Working Days with baby

I began cleaning houses to make extra money. I had two houses in Wenonah, NJ. One was a retired doctor and his wife, who treated me like their own. They moved to South Jersey from Princeton, NJ, and were a very wealthy couple. The house was newly built and adorned with beautiful antiques. I also began cleaning their daughter's house who was married to the Mayor of Wenonah. They lived in a large, beautiful, historic colonial home with impressive curb appeal, decorated in an elegant Williamsburg Colonial style. The house was massive—far too big to clean in a single day! I'd guess it was at least 4,500 square feet.

I was directed to clean the 1st floor one week and the second floor the next. I can recall having to take a lunch break to go to my mother's, who was babysitting Kristin, to feed her. The 3rd house I cleaned was a modern-style home with large glass windows surrounding the entire house. This family raised goats and had dogs and cats in the house. This was an all-day job. I remember sneezing my head off the entire time, and my eyes would tear and itch because I was allergic to cats! This house was close to my parent's home, so my mother would drive Kristin to the house, so I could breast feed her. Then take her back to her house, where I would pick her up when I finished.

When Kristin had her 5-month checkup with her pediatrician, it was discovered she was losing weight. This is never a good thing for an infant. So, her doctor suggested I give her formula and stop breastfeeding. However, he wanted me to give her formula from a baby cup, no bottle! He felt that would just create another takeaway a few months later. I was hesitant to try the baby cup, but to my amazement, Kristin handled the transition like a champ and began thriving and gaining weight. She was eating baby food, and her favorite was sweet potatoes and plums. She was always a step ahead in her development; at only 9 months old, she took her first steps.

Within a week, she was climbing out of her crib and we had to purchase a toddler bed and put a safety gate on her bedroom doorway. Within two weeks, she was climbing over the gate, and we had to add another gate on top. The scariest time was when she fell and had a hairline fracture in her skull and had to be hospitalized for 2 days. She certainly gave me a run for my money!

Early one morning, when she was 16 months old, she pulled the shelf down that was set on the back of the toilet. It was filled with my perfumes and her father's colognes. Luckily, she was never cut from the broken bottles. She was okay, with the exception of smelling like she was a swan in a sea of perfume! Unfortunately, this was not the end of Kristin's adventures and trips to the hospital.

When she was two, my parents kept her for a weekend while I was going to Wildwood with my friends, and her dad was working. She was sleeping between them in the middle of their king-size bed. She woke up early and decided she was getting up. Because my mother is a very light sleeper, Kristin crawled on her belly to the bottom of the bed and found her way to, once again, more danger! She quietly found her way to the kitchen reached up on the counter, and pulled a bottle of algaecide that the lid was not tightly sealed on her head! The algaecide burned her face and eyes! My mother woke up from her screaming and immediately threw her in the bathtub and flushed her eyes. My father called the ambulance and then called me. I never drove home from Wildwood so fast in my life! The doctor in the hospital said, had my mother not reacted so quickly, she could have lost her sight! Thank God for my mother's quick thinking. Once again, God Blessed us.

Our next-door neighbors were Daryl and Barbara. Gary worked all the time and would come home at night and be too tired to do anything. After I made friends with Barbara, she and I shared shopping trips and nights out to various pubs where we would drink beer and dance the night away. Barbara had a three-year-old son, who would come over and talk my ears off and entertain

29

Kristin with all his stories. In 1983, she and I decided we would get pregnant, and our babies could grow up together.

At the time, Gary and I still suffered from intimacy problems, and, for the record, we had marital problems I wasn't sure could be fixed. On May 5, 1983, my grandmother, my mother's mother, passed away! It was on this day that I realized I had no grandparents! It was very hard on my mother. There was nothing I could do to console her.

By the end of May 1983, Barbara told me she was pregnant. It was then I decided Gary and I would seek professional help so that I, too, could be pregnant. As they say, the pain of childbirth is forgotten with time. It was on the day that would have been my grandmother's 89th birthday, August 6, 1983, the day I conceived my second child. I experienced a bit of morning sickness, but only in the mornings, and after three months, this pregnancy would prove to be a breeze. I felt fine, and I was given a due date of May 2nd. Again, no ultrasound, so I had no idea what sex I was having.

I did not go to Dr Iceberg this time, but rather to a kind and very nice obstetrician, Dr. Gall. It was predetermined that I would be receiving an epidural and not suffer like I did with Kristin.

On February 29, 1984, my friend Barbara had a baby girl named Lisa. It wasn't until March that my husband and I decided we were going to move to a bigger house before our baby was born. We sold the little house in Clayton and actually made a decent amount of money to put down on a bigger L-shaped rancher in Williamstown, NJ. It was only five miles from the old house and close enough to stay in contact with Barbara.

I would begin babysitting in my home rather than cleaning houses since I was pregnant and had a home big enough to bring children into my home. It proved to be a better situation. This would start the beginning of my relationship with my friend Becky. She lived in my neighborhood, and she brought her two daughters, Jessica, 10, and Nicolette, 3, to my home Monday- Friday, where I would babysit them and be home with Kristin.

House and Baby # 2

We were still putting things away and getting the baby's room painted and ready when I felt my first contraction. It was a Tuesday afternoon, May 2nd, 1984. Should have learned that babies rarely come on their due dates, but my husband was off (Mondays and Tuesdays were his wonderful days off)! So, he drove me to the hospital to find out it was a false alarm and only Braxton-Hicks contractions. We would end up making another trip to the hospital on May 3rd at midnight to be once again sent home. I was only 1 centimeter dilated, and with my history of long labor, Dr. thought I'd be more comfortable at home. That comfort was very short-lived because the contractions were getting to be more than I cared to bear.

Back to the hospital for the 3rd time! This time, only 2 centimeters, but Dr decided to keep me, and once again, I was given an IV with Pitocin to speed up the process. However, Dr Gall, unlike Dr. Iceberg, accompanied the Pitocin with an epidural so the pain would be gone! What a relief to not feel the hard and active labor that was occurring.

Exactly 24 hours later, on May 5, 1984, at 2:16 AM, my second daughter was born! She cut 10 hours off my first labor. She had light brownish hair but not as much as Kristin, she weighed in at 8lbs and 1 oz. and she was 20" long. We named her Erin Marie; Erin was conceived on August 6th (my grandmother's would have been her 89th birthday) and was born on the day she passed 1 year later!

Marie was my grandmother's name. She was my second blessing, and we were on cloud nine, bringing her home. Typical that Erin held out till May 5th! Erin was a mild-mannered baby with no colic, and she was what was known as an easy baby. That is up until she had her 1st set of immunizations, she stopped breathing, and I had to call the paramedics to come to the house! It was determined she was allergic to Pertussis, one of the three medications in the DPT immunization. Pertussis is given to prevent a whopping cough. However, Erin would not receive another DPT. She would only get DT shots from that time on. When Erin was only a month old, she was having bloody stools, and it was then the Dr. told us she may be allergic to cow's milk formula. Since I decided not to nurse Erin due to my past experience with Kristin. Not wanting to make the same mistake twice, I bottle-fed, never thinking this would be a problem. However, back in 1984, formula without cow's milk was very expensive!

During this time, the only drug store that carried this special formula was Thrift Drugs, it was only sold in a powder concentrate and had no preservatives, therefore could only be made per serving. It was called Nutramigen. It cost $27.00/ a can, which in 1984 was very expensive.

It was then that I made the decision I needed to make more money than what I could make babysitting. My marriage was deteriorating, so I went to bartending school. After graduating from the class, I got a job as a bartender, working nights at Glass Bowl Bowling Alley. A few months later, I was offered a job at P&B diner as the first bartender to open this new diner with a bar. I worked there for a few months until they wanted me to work days; this would infringe on my babysitting, so that ended my job at P&B Diner.

It was then my marriage was also done! My husband moved to Margate because he worked in Atlantic City as a Craps Floorperson. We just were not seeing eye to eye, and we were living more like brother and sister than a married couple. So, I remained in the house in Williamstown and got a job at Liberty Bell Tavern to make ends meet. I would babysit Monday- Friday, 7 AM till 5 PM, and then I worked at Liberty Bell Tavern in Malaga, NJ, on Friday and Saturday nights from 10 PM until 5 AM! I hired a babysitter for my two girls for two nights a week.

I began living a single life, going out with Denise to pubs and nightclubs. Our favorite spot was Thursday nights at Schooner's Inn in Woodbury Heights. We had so many great times there. I met and dated a few guys, but nothing ever got serious. I was awaiting a court date for my divorce and living day to day, doing the best I could to be a mother of two girls.

In October of 1985 my parents won a small lottery and lent me $4000. to put an addition on my house. The girls were getting bigger, and so were their toys. Between bikes, scooters, balls, wagons, etc., we were in need of a garage. So, I began getting prices from local contractors. After about 3 estimates, I hired a company called "Universal Home Improvements." The owner, Lou was very nice, and he gave me the most reasonable estimate, but he gave me more than that, his foreman on my job, who would become my second husband!

Prince Charming Arrives

It was a Thursday evening in November of 1986 when Lou brought my contract to sign for my addition. My parents came over for support. My best friend Denise and I were going to Schooner's Inn after the contract was signed; my parents would stay to babysit the girls. Lou brought his foreman with him to see the property, as he would be doing the work.

I will never forget the first time I laid eyes on him. He came into my house wearing an insulated hunter-green one-piece winter jumpsuit. He stood 6ft 2" tall, had dark hair with a beard and mustache, and piercing green eyes. Absolutely ruggedly handsome! He reminded me of a dark version of Jeremiah Johnson. He got my attention immediately! His smile was full of sparkle, and his personality was friendly. My parents asked most of the questions since they were well versed in construction; after all the questions were answered, I signed the contract, and construction would begin on Black Friday.

While Denise and I drove to Schooner's Inn, it was all I could talk about: this handsome contractor who was going to put the addition on my home. On Friday, November 28, 1986, at 8:00 AM, there was a knock on my front door. I opened the door to Prince Charming, who asked me if my mother was home. I said, "I am the mother." he laughed and said Oh, I'm sorry, I thought you were the older daughter; you look so young. I assumed he was trying to flatter me, but he really thought my mother was the homeowner because of all her questions. He had no idea that I was the homeowner and that I had two daughters. He told me they were going to start setting up and that the heavy equipment would be digging for the addition. The grass would need to be ripped out, and they would begin stringing lines for the addition. It was also decided that for a couple thousand dollars more, I could have a dining room as well as a garage added. So, he would be turning my L-shaped rancher into a U-shaped rancher.

As my excitement grew over my addition, it also grew over my contractor. I began bringing hot coffee out to all three of the workers every morning. One morning, I was asked by my foreman where my husband was. I explained we were separated and getting a divorce. From that day on, everything began to change. He smiled at me more, and every day, when he brought back my coffee cups, he would chat with me more and more.

He started talking to my daughters and the two girls I babysat. He was a real charmer. By the end of the second week of December, the concrete was laid and ready for framing, and then we had a giant snowstorm! My job was at a halt for at least 10-12 days! I didn't see my contractor at all until I ran around the corner to Cumberland Farms to grab a gallon of milk, and he pulled in next to me to pick up a cheesesteak from Milanos Pizza, which was right next to the Cumberland Farms. Not sure what made me do this, but I asked him if I could cook dinner for him one night? Unlike me, to be that bold, but there you go, it was done. He smiled and said sure, we would talk about it on January 2nd when he came back to work.

I continued babysitting and working at Liberty Bell Tavern. Kristin was now 5 and in kindergarten at Radix Elementary, so during the morning hours, it was just Nicolette and Erin. Kristin would get home shortly after 12 noon and Jessica after 3 PM. On January 2nd, when the contractors came back, we picked a date for our dinner plans. Wednesday, January 7, 1987, I would prepare lasagna for my Prince. After they wrapped up the day at my house, my contractor went home to shower and change clothes and came back for our 1st date. It couldn't have gone better; the girls seemed to get along with him, and he played games with them while I cleaned up the kitchen. Later that night, after the girls were tucked in their beds, we shared our first kiss. It was full of passion and excitement. This would begin our whirlwind romance.

My friend Linda who lived next door, who I frequently spent most of my time with, had us over to her house for dinner so she could meet him. Her husband Jim seemed to get along well with my new Prince, as they talked about the construction of my addition, as well as what renovations Jim was doing with his house. Linda and Jim had no children and had desperately tried to have a child. Linda suffered from endometriosis and, even taking fertility drugs, was unable to conceive. Linda and Jim adopted a baby girl they named Nicole because they picked her up from the hospital a few days before Christmas.

They were living on cloud nine for approximately one month when the birth mother changed her mind, and they had to give the baby back. I remember going to her house and removing everything that was in the house for the baby. I packed everything in my garage so Linda did not have a single reminder that there was ever a baby in the house. It was a very sad time. I had planned a Valentine's Dinner that my Prince failed to show up for.

I can clearly remember feeling the anger and disappointment when I never even received a phone call till days later! He showed up like nothing happened with some crazy story about getting stuck in another state from another snowstorm. It didn't sound plausible to me, and I was contemplating just forgetting about him. However, I decided I'd be patient and see what happens. By April, my addition was done, and my Prince still kept coming around.

By June of 1987, he started spending the weekends at my house. By the end of July, he was there more than he was at his house. My court date for my divorce was coming close, and my prince was still keeping close, but I had no commitment. On August 30, 1987, I drove to the Court House in Woodbury, NJ, where I would officially become a divorced woman! So, exactly 7 years to the day! I was officially a free woman. Isn't it ironic, to be married and divorced on the same day? Life was good for the most part; however, I was torn by the lifestyle I was living.

I had two beautiful daughters and practically a live-in boyfriend. I felt truly in love with my prince, who was redoing our house for free: new carpets, fresh paint, a chair railing added to our family room, and wallpaper in my dining room. You name it, he could do it, and I was amazed at his carpentry skills. By

September, he had almost every room in my house renovated to some degree. I still continued to babysit but I had given up my bartending job and took on another little girl to babysit. This little girl was the same age as Erin; her name was Heather. Her mother, Gina, met my ex-husband, and the two of them began dating.

After a month, the situation became uncomfortable for all involved, and Gina decided to take Heather elsewhere for care. Shortly after Heather left, Nicolette and my daughter Erin decided to give me the scare of my life! I was carrying groceries in the house; the two little mischievous girls decided to undo the belts on the car seats and run down the street and through the drainage ditch to Nicolette's house. When I came back outside within a minute, and they were not in the car seats, I started calling their names, and when I got no answer, I checked inside the house; at first, I just assumed they were hiding. But as my heart was beating out of control, and they were not inside or outside, I called the Police! I thought someone must have kidnapped them! I called my ex-husband, as well as my boyfriend, and Nicolette's Mother, Becky, at work. The police arrived in minutes, and after about five minutes, I was told an officer found them at Nicolette's house, sitting on steps inside her house, eating cookies and candy!!!! OMG! Although I was relieved, they were okay, I was furious at the same time!

That was a lesson of motherhood that I never wanted to repeat! Erin & Nicolette were both punished, and from that day forward, never ever out of my sight for a minute.

Two weddings!

It was in the Fall on October 2, 1987. It was on a Friday night, during a candlelight wedding service at Incarnation Church in Mantua, NJ, the same church I was married in 7 years earlier, that my sister became a married woman! Both my girls were flower girls in the ceremony, and I was her Maid of Honor. It was a beautiful ceremony, and my Prince was with me.

My daughters were adorned in beautiful white eyelet gowns with pink ribbons that my mother made. My sister had a beautiful white gown with a veil attached to the halo that wrapped around her head. She was a beautiful bride, and the wedding was so beautiful. Her reception was directly followed at Mazzo's in Glassboro, NJ. Her reception was wonderful, and the best part of the reception was when my Prince proposed to me! It was not a typical proposal where he got down on one knee and chattered a bunch of words like "I love you! Will you marry me"? It was on the dance floor when we were slow dancing, and he said... "You look so beautiful in this white and black laced dress that how about we go get married tonight?"

I laughed, and he said, "I'm serious!" I was stunned but knew that I was not going to get married that night. My youngest daughter was sleeping on chairs at a table, and my oldest daughter was tired, too. So, as we sat at the table having a drink, he persisted with this idea of us planning to elope.

As much as I knew in my heart that he was my Prince Charming, I also knew that I had only been officially divorced for 33 days! There wasn't a question about how I felt for him, but more about getting married again so soon. By the end of the night, I was convinced that it would be better to raise my children in a home with the stability of marriage than to raise them in a home where their mother had a live-in boyfriend.

The following day, we went to the mall to look for wedding rings. My Prince bought a suit, and I had already purchased a beautiful ankle-length ivory-laced dress that I had found on a sales rack a few months prior. However, the dilemma was how I was going to get this dress that was being stored in my mother's closet at my mother's house without my mother's knowledge.

So, I stopped by to visit with my girls, and while my mother was preparing a snack in the kitchen, I quietly snuck back into her bedroom, snatched the dress, and threw it in my large purse. Then I decided also to borrow my mother's pretty ivory leather heels and threw them in my bag, and ran outside to my car. We also had to concoct a story on why I needed my mother to keep the girls for 5 days. We decided to say we were going to the Poconos with friends. I hated lying to my mother, but what else could I do? We had so many things to iron out, time off of work for both of us, and arrangements and reservations. We did it all in a week's time! My Prince even put a roof on his uncle's house in Franklinville, NJ, to have extra money to afford everything! Everything was planned and ready except for the fact that I still never met my future in-laws! It was a nagging issue for me to marry a man whom I have never met his parents!

So, on October 13, 1987, we were on our journey, which started out by stopping by the homestead of my future in-laws. When we pulled up to a house that was set 50 feet from the railroad tracks and looked like a house that was crying for paint and renovations, I was in a state of wow! Especially when the front door was unlocked! We stepped into a kitchen with a linoleum floor so worn that there were patches where the plywood was visible.

The kitchen table was cluttered with everything from paperwork to a slab of butter left from a prior meal. He led me through the dining room and into the living room, but the house was empty! His mother and father were not at home. So, short of meeting the dog, the trip to his parent's house was unproductive and very disappointing for me. I would be marrying my prince without ever meeting his parents.

The next stop would be at a motel in Delaware. We went to a pub and had drinks and ate dinner then went back to the motel to sleep. We got up early the next day and continued our journey to Maryland to apply for our marriage license. There would be a 3-day wait!

On the way back, we ate at a really quaint restaurant in Maryland that reminded me of something you would see down South in Tennessee, where everyone was so friendly and spoke with a southern drawl. It was a true adventure, sight-seeing through Maryland and just enjoying each other's company. It was a beautiful trip, and the Best was yet to come.

We got up early on Friday, October 16, 1987. It was a bright, warm, sunny day in October. Not a cloud in the sky! We picked up our marriage license and drove to an elegant stone church on a cobblestone road in Elkton, Maryland, where a lady minister with the same hairstyle as I had would marry us! The organ played the traditional wedding song as I walked into the room on a white paper runner to my Prince. It was a short but sweet ceremony; however, it was official! I was now married and would become the wife of my Prince Harry!!! Imagine that? It was a little over a month ago. I was married to Gary, and now I was married to Harry!!!! How's that for iconic?

After our wedding, we headed to the Poconos in Pennsylvania. It was a long ride from Maryland, but we had a great time; stopping to eat, coupled with a few restrooms stops, we made it by mid-afternoon. As soon as we arrived, we had photographs taken in our wedding wear, which were taken on a bridge with beautiful fall foliage in the background. It was so beautiful, with the leaves changing and the wooded scenery. We had a cabin on top of a hill in the woods with a built-in swimming pool inside. We had a room service dinner with a bottle of champagne to celebrate!

As I lay on our huge king-size bed, exhausted but exhilarated by the wild yet tender love we shared, I was so happy and grateful that, for the first time in my life, I felt like a woman who not only loved but was loved deeply and tenderly by a man. It is hard to believe that we had our first date only nine months ago, and he is now my husband. I felt fulfilled and content. Everything was so different and so exciting that I was in a state of Bliss. We spent four days of pure happiness on top of a hill in a cabin with deer roaming the woods and skinny dipping in our pool. This was a honeymoon I would never forget. We did leave the resort to go site seeing one day, and we did eat in the resort restaurant one night; we played Miniature Golf one day, and Harry taught me how to play pool, but the majority of our honeymoon was spent alone in our cabin on top of the hill in the woods. I hated to see it end.

The News

We had big news to share upon returning home, my parents were pretty surprised when we revealed we were married! I explained how I had secretly taken my ivory lace dress and borrowed her shoes from the closet, returning them now without her knowing. But my ex-husband had gotten upset, which then made my oldest daughter, who was only six at the time, upset as well. My youngest daughter, being only three, didn't care but asked why she couldn't be the flower girl at our wedding like she was at Aunt Kelly's wedding.

Trying to explain what elopement meant to children was challenging, and why we couldn't have a traditional wedding because both of us had been married and divorced; therefore, we decided to just run away and get married. Harry finally took me to meet his parents and, in the process, introduced me as his wife. His mother was very receptive and welcomed me to the family. However, his father said, "Wife! What happened to the other bitch you had been dating?" His father was known to be a bit rough around the edges.

In time, everyone seemed to accept our marriage, and things calmed down, but we had some unfinished business to attend to, such as selling Harry's house since he was now living with us full-time. We decided to wait until after the holidays to put his house on the market. Meantime, the Christmas spirit was in high gear when Harry came home and surprised me with a Live Christmas tree. I only had a live Christmas tree once in my life! Growing up, my parents always had an artificial tree, except for my 16th birthday, when the only gift I asked for was a real Christmas Tree! That was the only live Christmas Tree I ever remembered decorating. Harry coming home with a live tree for our 1st Christmas as a married couple was another glimpse of my validation for my husband.

On New Year's Eve, we spent at home with the girls. We allowed them to bang pots and pans at midnight. We were truly a happy family. I enrolled in the LPN program at Gloucester County Vocational School, and in 15 months, I could become a Licensed Practical Nurse. In mid-February, I surprised my husband with the best Valentine's Day Gift; we were going to have a baby!!!! We briefly talked about it, and he definitely wanted to expand our family. He was ecstatic when I gave him the news. I was pregnant! Our baby would be due on October 26, 1988. So, the family was growing, and we began talking about selling both houses and buying a bigger home. I always wanted to move back to my childhood town in Sewell NJ, where I held the most wonderful memories. So, we decided after the baby arrived, we would be looking for a new home together.

Things were good, and life was full of joy. Until mid-September, when I entered the Acme in Williamstown to shop and slipped in smashed fruit and water on the floor and went down hard on my left knee! I filled out the accident report even though I thought I was uninjured; I was almost 8 months pregnant at the time.

By nightfall, my knee was swelled up three sizes bigger than my right knee. Being pregnant, I could not get an X-ray, so I decided not to go to the hospital. I iced it and watched it, and eventually, the swelling decreased. But, on the downside, I was missing school at the time when I was supposed to be going to the hospital to learn through practical, hands-on experience. With the pregnancy and swelled knee and being told I would have to wait and start all over from the beginning again, I quit! The timing was just not right; in 6 weeks, I'd be giving birth to a brand-new baby.

Now I could relax and get my nesting underway, preparing the nursery and getting everything in order. Little did I know that it would be a short relaxation period because a couple of days later, I woke up getting labor pains 6 weeks too soon! Harry drove me to West Jersey Hospital, and I was given medication through an IV called Tocolytics. After a couple of hours, the contractions stopped, and we went home.

On October 16th, our 1st wedding anniversary, I was as big as a hippo; at least it felt like I was that and moving like a turtle. As my due date grew closer, I began spotting, something that I never experienced with the two prior pregnancies. I went to see the, Dr. Who said I was beginning to deface but not dilated at all. So, when October 26th came and went with no delivery, I was not surprised.

On Halloween, I walked the girls all through the neighborhood, filling their bags with candy and treats and hoping it would bring on labor. No luck because when I revisited the Dr. On November 1st, she just said the baby will come when the baby is ready. So, you can imagine how disappointed I felt; I was now almost a week past my due date with not a single contraction or pain.

On November 2nd, as I climbed into bed at 11 PM, it hit me like a ton of bricks!!!! There were no ifs, ands, or buts; that was a contraction that took my breath away! There would be no sleep tonight because baby number 3 was on the way. I had lost my mucus plug a week earlier, and now the contractions were strong, lasting long, and coming about five minutes apart. After my husband called the doctor, he was advised to bring me to the hospital once the contractions were three minutes apart. Now, mind you, the hospital was 35 minutes away, and I had this awful insurance called HIP of NJ, and I would be delivering baby number 3 at West Jersey Hospital in Vorhees, NJ.

It was a grueling night, and at 6:30 AM, my mother arrived to care for the girls and hospital-bound we were. My water broke on the way, another detail different from my two prior births where the Dr would have to break my water. Upon examination, I was only 3 centimeters dilated, so they had me walking the halls of the maternity ward. By noon, I had an epidural because the pain was too much to bear. When this Dr walked in and told me he'd be delivering my baby, I thought, of course, my least favorite of the 6 obstetricians in practice would be the Dr. on call to deliver my baby. In the late 80's, hospitals began delivering babies in hospital rooms. So, I wasn't getting carted to a delivery room and put on a cold metal table this time. However, when I was ready to push, Dr. Gewirtz came into my room, and while I was trying not to push, panting like a dog, he looked at me and said…" do you mind if I change the channel on your TV, my story is on"?

OMG!!!! In between pushes, he was engrossed in the Guiding Light; yes, the Dr. was watching a soap opera. After about 5 pushes, the nurse caught my son, who flew out of me like a bullet! Dr.Gewirtz looks at the nurse and says," Great Catch."!

So, The Prince and I had a son! He was born on November 3, 1988, at 2:58 PM. He was 8 lbs. and 10 ounces, 21 inches long, and screaming his head off! He was covered in a cheesy film from head to toe, and his skin was peeling like a snake. He was taken to the special nursery. The Dr said this sometimes happens when a baby is over-baked, which basically means past the due date. The name we picked out for a boy was Kevin. However, my husband decided he wanted a junior, so he would be Harry Jr. We were told after his circumcision he had a clotting problem. The Dr had a hard time stopping the bleeding after the procedure. He was known as the stud of the nursery! The nurses would tell us he was very well endowed, which, for me, growing up with one sister and no brothers, I wouldn't know. After three days, we were both released from the hospital, happy and supposedly healthy.

The Bloody Truth

We arrived home on November 6, 1988, with our new bundle of joy. I was once again trying the breast feeding. He seemed to have taken to it with less struggle than my daughter, and he was always screaming except when I nursed him. My husband would carry him around the house to calm him, but as soon as he put him down, he would begin crying. Unlike my girls, he had very little hair; in fact, he looked bald with a very light blonde peach fuzz and had big blue eyes. He was a beautiful baby boy but not a happy baby. In the midst of trying to cope with him, I had my two daughters, who were 7 and 4, to care for.

On top of all this, I didn't feel well. I was bleeding like a slaughtered pig, and I just didn't feel right. I did not remember feeling this way after having my girls. I knew it was normal to get a period after giving birth, but this was different. I was changing a sanitary napkin every hour, and for the record, in 1987, sanitary napkins were big, bulky, and thick, unlike the thin, flat pads they make today. My point is I was losing a lot of blood! I was so tired and had barely enough energy to fake motherhood. When I went back to the Dr. For my two-week check-up, I was told I was on my feet too much, and I needed to slow down so that my bleeding would stop. How was I going to slow down- my husband went back to work, and I had to take care of my children.

As the days turned into weeks, I was growing weaker, and the bleeding never stopped! One morning, I got up and got the girls off to school. Kristin was in 1st grade, but Erin was only in preschool for a half day. I came home from dropping them off, and I put Baby Harry in the swing, and that is all I remember. Thank God for my neighbor Linda, who came over and found me on the living room floor; I had passed out! She got me up, and I called my husband to come home to take me to the hospital. Linda picked up Erin from preschool, and my mother came over to be with the girls. After testing, it was determined that my placenta had broken down prior to my son's birth, and pieces were still left in my uterus.

So, I was admitted to the hospital and was given a D&C to remove the pieces of placenta, and then I was put on intervenes antibiotics. So much for HIP of NJ Healthcare and good old Dr Gewirtz. I had a blood infection known as sepsis from my placenta that became dead tissue after being left behind from delivery. This was a nightmare that should have never happened.

Furthermore, I was breastfeeding my son, which probably was not good for him. My husband had to begin bottle feeding him because I spent two weeks in the hospital, and my milk basically dried up during the recovery. I sensed that something was off, yet I trusted the doctor who assured me I was fine. If I could offer anyone advice on something important, it would be to trust your intuition, as it's often accurate. I suffered for two and half weeks from Septic poisoning, which is a serious blood infection that really could have caused my death had I waited much longer to get to the hospital. This would mark my first experience of having mistrust in the medical field. After coming home from the hospital, believing I was well, and the trauma of my ordeal was over, I tried to get back in the swing of things, doing as much of my normal routine as possible. Imagine how I felt when I realized that the worst was yet to come.

After 6 weeks, my husband and I returned to a long overdue rendezvous that was complete with a couple of beers and a romantic dinner. Perfect evening with all the romance. However, that evening would prove to be a lesson beyond all lessons! About two weeks later, I began my period, which was heavy and very painful. Basically, here we go again! I continued to bleed, and then I began passing gray tissue. I decided to go back to the hospital for the second time in 8 weeks. Come to find out, I was still passing placental tissue, and I would have to endure another D&C!

However, this time, I would also be having a laparoscopic surgery so the Dr could see how much tissue was still in my uterus. I still recall waking to severe pain in my stomach and chest, but the real pain came when the Dr disclosed that I was pregnant again and unfortunately lost the baby with the D&C. How pathetic can the medical field be? How can one person make this many mistakes? I was devastated! How did I get pregnant after one time? OMG! I felt like my prince and I were not getting our fairytale life. I can remember being so sad and so angry at the same time.

During the recovery round two, we decided to put his house and my house on the market. We needed a fresh start. After two weeks, Harry's house sold, and we were close to selling my house. The house where it all started, the house he did so much work to, the house where we celebrated all our firsts. The house where I served him coffee and burnt Christmas cookies while the addition went up. It would now belong to a new family. So, we were out looking at houses every chance we got. It was an early evening. One day, we were coming home from my parent's house, and there it was! The house that made us turn around to see.

It was a remodeled farmhouse with a big country porch big enough to catch my eye. It was on an acre plus of land and was equipped with a tire swing in the backyard. Perfect for our children. Holy Moly! Yes, Virginia, there is a Santa Claus!! It was so perfect for us that we had our realtor show us the house the very next day. The funny thing about this house was the realtor who sold both our homes, was the listing agent on this home too. So, it was all too easy: we put the offer in and started packing… we were moving to Barnsboro, NJ, very close to my favorite childhood home. I was moving back to the town where the best of my childhood memories lived. Maybe we would get that fairytale life after all.

Barnsboro Family hits the Frontpage

We had two settlements on July 30, 1989. The sale of my Williamstown home and the purchase of our Barnsboro home. By 1 pm, we had accomplished all the legalities and were handed the key to our dream home. Luckily for us, the family that purchased our home allowed us to go back to the house and move our furniture; they were not moving in right away. This allowed us to make several trips with the U-Haul truck to our new home. We needed to paint rooms, amongst other things, but we were moving in.

We have forever to transition. We got the beds set up so we would have sleeping arrangements in place. Hooked up our refrigerator, washer, and dryer, brought boxes in, and tried to put them in the perspective rooms. Then came the fun part. We were dirty, and we all needed to bathe for bed. I went up to the bathroom to fill the tub for the girls so they could get cleaned and ready for bed. When I tell you that when I turned on the water, I barely got a drip, that would not be an exaggeration! Drip, Drip, Drip, and then Nothing!!! Well, I quickly ran downstairs to try the kitchen faucet, then the powder room, and to my dismay, we had absolutely no running water! The very next day, we called our realtor about the problem. She came over and verified that we had no running water in the home and that she just sold us less than 24 hours ago. She went back to her broker, who pretty much wrote us off and told us in so many words…. It was our problem.

Our problem? My ass!!!! I contacted the Gloucester County Times Newspaper, and the next day, we were on our beautiful country front porch posing for our picture, which would make the Front Page of the newspaper the very next day! "Family Left High and Dry with No Water after Making Settlement on their Dream Home" So again, we would experience a not-so-happy ending.

However, there was a bright side when Cloister Water Company brought us cases of bottled water the day after our picture appeared in the paper. My beautiful porch was covered with cases upon cases of water! In the midst of our dilemma, we learned that the family who lived in the house before us was experiencing a lack of water but never disclosed it to the realtor or us.

We went to see an attorney to learn our rights and what we should do. We put every penny we saved, along with the monies from the sale of our homes, down on this dream house that had a water well that dried up! This was not something that happens every day; in fact, it never happens! But it happened to us, and on top of having no water in the home, it was early August, and during an unconventional, very hot spell, we had no air conditioning, so we were hot, sweaty, and irritable. I also learned that my husband tried to throw a load of wash in earlier that afternoon to test that he hooked it up properly, and because there was no water, it burned the motor up in my washing machine.

What were we to do? Well, we drove to my parent's house to shower and wash our clothes. And we ate out a whole hell of a lot! After our lawyer sent letters threatening a lawsuit to the broker, our realtor, and the well driller who installed the well only 4 years prior to our purchase, we were happy to learn that Delsea Well Drilling would drill us a brand new well, free of charge! As far as our realtor goes, she escaped unharmed, however we would Never use her services ever again! As far as the broker, we made sure to put him under the bus every chance we had. It was an ordeal we would never forget, and the lesson learned is never to use a realtor who is working for both sides, you cannot work honestly for the seller and buyer simultaneously. Eventually, the laws changed, and this would never happen in today's world. We decided that one day, we would both get our Real Estate Licenses to ensure this problem would never happen to anyone else.

We got our new well, and we had water. Unfortunately, the water smelled like sulfur; every time I turned the water on, the scent of rotten eggs would fragrant the room. To make matters worse, the iron levels were so high that the toilets and sinks were orange. Forget trying to wear white; even bleached whites looked gray. It was not what we expected, but we continued painting, wallpapering, and stenciling.

The house was a beautiful country farmhouse with beautiful decor. I stenciled pineapples above a chair rail in my living room, all the high woodwork was painted a beautiful French blue, and the kitchen and dining area were mauve and blue. My husband remodeled the attic into a beautiful bedroom for Kristin. It was wonderful, all was wonderful until I began noticing that our son was not meeting his milestones. He was delayed in speech and was very disciplined about his blankets, toys, and even his socks on his feet. He was not affectionate and did not like to be hugged or kissed. Basically, he did not like being touched. He grunted and pointed even after he was over a year old. I mentioned my concerns to the pediatrician; he said Well, if he doesn't start talking by two years of age, I will send him for tests. My husband kept saying he would be fine; you are used to girls; boys are slower than girls. So that was that he was going to be fine. He was going to be fine, but was I?

Staff photo

Dana Frye and kids Harry Jr., 9 months, Kristin 8, and Erin, 5, stand outside of their home, which has

there's just no way we can afford it.   garden hose from the basement of   for the children —

Going Under the Knife

We were just getting settled in our new home, and things were running pretty smoothly until I was coming down the steps one morning when my knee locked, and I could not bend it. I was walking on the balls of my toes on my left foot for a few days before I went to the hospital. My knee was swollen like a cantaloupe, and I could not straighten it out. The hospital took an X-ray and referred me to an orthopedic surgeon. At Jefferson Hospital, I met with the surgeon, who asked how the injury had happened. I explained that I was walking down the stairs when my left knee suddenly locked. "Well," he said, "you must have recently hit it or fell on it or some sort of accident to injure your knee." No matter what I said, I could not convince him. He believed I had a torn cartilage that was causing my issue, so he scheduled laparoscopic surgery for the next day. It was outpatient surgery, and I would be in and out in 1 day.

I had only 2 surgeries in my life; the first was having my tonsils and adenoids removed at age 5. The second was a D&C to remove the pieces of placenta that were left in my uterus after my son's birth. As Harry drove me to the hospital the next morning, I was scared to death! I was hoping my son Harry was going to be good for my mother and father, and he wouldn't be screaming all day. The next thing I remember was waking up and not feeling my left leg. The Surgeon came in with the bad news. "Well, you were right about not doing anything recently to hurt your knee because this was an old injury that has caused the tibia bone to begin to die; the bad news is that you cannot go home today because we had to remove a half dollar sized broken bone that was dislodged off your tibia and got stuck in your knee joint. The sand dollar-shaped bone was too large to go through the scope. Therefore, we had to cut across your knee to open it up enough to remove the bone. Then we had to drill your tibia and femur bone in your leg to regenerate new blood flow to keep the bones from continuing to die."

All I could do was cry. Why does everything always turn out worse than the doctors say? They gave me pain meds to ease the throbbing, and I was able to go home the next day after they removed the drain. I was sent home on crutches and a prescription for pain meds and physical therapy. I hated the way the pain meds made me feel tired and nauseous, so I only took them at bedtime and when I had to go to physical therapy. The place Harry would have to take me twice a week was all the way in Medford, NJ; it couldn't be somewhere close and more convenient. It was a jaunt to Medford from Barnsboro twice a week.

This HIP of NJ insurance was again letting me down! It was a long, grueling few months, and after it was over, I filed a lawsuit against Acme Market in Williamstown. This injury was from my fall in the Acme when I was 8 months pregnant and did not seek medical care because I couldn't get an X-ray due to my pregnancy. The lawyer I hired was Neil Axe from Slifken & Axe Law firm. This lawsuit would drag on for 2 years before it would settle, and I was awarded $25,000. Not enough to compensate for having surgery and all my pain and agony. The money went into my bank account to start my daycare business.

Kiddie Korral was Born

My husband was doing construction but for a new contractor. He would have slow times and would not have work, which meant no paycheck. This was starting to cause financial stress as we had 3 children now, a new home, and a mortgage, and my only income was the child support I received from my Ex. Which at the time was not much. I didn't want to go out of the house to work and have to put my son in daycare. So, the solution was to go back to babysitting.

In 1989, it was not legal to babysit without a license, so I went through Gloucester County Family Daycare, and after taking classes and passing a home inspection, I had a license to serve five children for a fee and three without a fee. Basically, allowing a caregiver three children of their own would not count in the five. I had a sign made out front after I decided on Kiddie Korral! The prince actually came up with the name. I was amazed at how fast I reached my five children quota; my first student would be Frankie, followed by Colleen, Christine, Brian, and Jessica. I had to continue taking classes and having unannounced inspections to ensure safety and quality care were being maintained.

After nine months, my husband was complaining about our home being turned into a daycare center. Toys were scattered all over the house, a changing table in our living room and cribs in our bedroom upstairs. Special food in our refrigerator that was only for the children, and he said we gotta do something to make this more accommodating for your business as well as our family.

So, the decision was made that I would apply for a business loan and if I could get it, the prince would put an addition on our Main St Home equipped with a bathroom for just my daycare children. I did everything right for once in my life. I had opened a business account under Kiddie Korral at United Jersey Bank and David was my loan officer. It went through without a hitch and with $25,000. I was able to put on a 550 square ft. addition with a full bathroom and office. The room was decorated with Big Bird, Bert and Ernie, and Cookie Monster.

Back in 1989, Sesame Street was hot! After the addition was completed and I began using it for the children, I had so many people calling and stopping by looking to enroll their child or children. I had a waiting list that I couldn't fulfill so it was then I looked into gaining a Full State License through the State of NJ Division of Child Services. Back in the day known as DYFS. There was a lot to do to achieve this status. I had taken nursing courses, child development courses, bartending, etc. but No Degree.

To get a Director's License through the State of NJ was one of the biggest achievements (besides my children) that I ever accomplished. There was so much paperwork, so much money, and so many inspections and requirements. I also had to be finger-printed and a complete background check; you might think I was becoming President of the United States! But it all went well; there were many hoops I had to jump, and I jumped everyone with vigor.

By January of 1990, I was a NJ State-Licensed Director, with a license for 12 children. The only thing I had to do was find an employee who would work with me. I called my friend Barbara, who was my first neighbor in my first house, and she agreed to come to work for me. The enrollment was fast and furious! I had established a good reputation, and by June of 1990, I had to hire another employee, Sheila, who would become known as Mom-Mom Sheila.

I had it worked out so that by 4:00 PM, I could retire for the day, and Barb and Sheila would work till 6:00 PM and close. It was long hours, 6:30 AM until 6:00 PM. With 12 children to care for and my own 3, you might know that I loved children! Everything was growing and going wonderful, but the way I've come to understand life, it's when things are going really well that the axe must fall. It was a Saturday afternoon, and I had dropped Kristin off at Clearview High School for her youth soccer practice. I was driving home when suddenly I felt a stabbing pain in my chest as if a knife had pierced through it!

By the time I got home, the pain was so severe that I entered my home and laid on the sofa. I couldn't yell for my husband, I couldn't cry, and breathing was a chore. I was experiencing the worst pain of my life- it was worse than childbirth, all 3 of them! It was indescribable pain that I thought I was going to die! This is where my story began in my prologue. This is when my husband rushed me to Underwood Hospital; this is when my life would never be the same.

This is when I would once again become a mystery to the world of medicine. This is when I experienced my 1st chest tube; this is when I was introduced to a life of pain. Pain that would haunt me for many years to come! I was 30 years old, married twice, and had two daughters and a son. I created a reputable and successful childcare center with two employees. I worked very hard, and my effort was rewarded, but now, as I lay in a hospital bed with a chest tube in my side and morphine being pumped into my veins, I can only wonder and pray that the doctor will be correct this time, and it was just a freak spontaneous pneumothorax that would never happen again.

Children's Hospital

Shortly after my hospital stay and return to work, the pediatrician ordered testing for Harry. We took him to Children's Hospital in South Philadelphia, where he was put to sleep for Brain Stem Testing. As we sat waiting for the doctor to come out and talk to us about the results, I prayed for a positive report.

Unfortunately, my prayers were not answered in the way I had hoped. The Neurologist told us that our son had severe brain damage to the upper left hemisphere of his brain and that he would never speak! OMG! Oh, how I cried. I cried all the way home, and I cried myself to sleep that night and many nights after. What caused this? Was it my fall in the supermarket? Was it the medicine given to me to stop early labor? Was it the placenta deteriorating while I carried him? Was it from breastfeeding him when I had septicemia? Was it our genes? We would never know!

As a licensed Director, I had many connections, so I quickly enrolled him in early intervention services. He was quite difficult to manage at this time. He would hit the children in my center, he would bang his head on the wall from frustration, he would suck his thumb to calm himself, and it was all I could do to pacify him and keep his anger under control. I actually enrolled him in a preschool up the street in hopes that would alleviate the stress of having him at my center. That didn't work, and he was suspended from the preschool after one week. Life was tough. My dream of having more children was slowly diminishing. Not knowing what caused his disability was a real killer. It was hard on everyone; he was almost impossible to live with.

Making matters worse were my monthly trips to the hospital with severe pain. Of course, the doctor was wrong; spontaneous pneumothorax could not be my problem; it was becoming a monthly trip to the emergency room where I would be given an X-ray and told I had another pneumothorax and needed another chest tube! It had gotten to be a monthly ritual with no diagnosis to be had! What the hell was happening to me? What was wrong with my son? How was I going to fix our current situation? The sadness was turning to despair. Somebody helps us!!!! Please, God, help my son- help me- we need your help. I would pray and go to church by myself every Sunday. Nobody else could help us, and my strength was found in God to help us.

When Harry turned 3, I enrolled him in a preschool handicapped program in the Mantua Township school system. He would go to school every day. A small bus would pick him up at 8:30 Am, and he would not return until 3:30 PM. He had two wonderful teachers, and both were named Tracy. They were the Best Teachers I ever knew. Tracy H was his classroom teacher, and Tracey J was his speech pathologist. Two wonderful and gifted teachers with the same name but spelled differently. When I tell you they were amazing, I mean absolutely AMAZING!

Harry spent two years with these wonderful ladies that helped him tremendously. It took away a lot of stress for our family. His time at home became more pleasurable, with fewer outbursts and temper tantrums. He still was not speaking but he was learning still the same. He had this very keen sense of hearing and would wake up in the middle of the night by a dog barking two houses away. It was a continual challenge with no answers and more questions every day. I would lie in bed at night, trying to figure out how to get answers.

One night, it finally dawned on me that I needed to find my birth mother to obtain my family's medical history. Perhaps this will be the light at the end of the tunnel. I began realizing that it wasn't just me anymore. Yes, I am sick, and yes, the doctors haven't been able to help me. But more importantly, I have 3 children, and my son with a medical issue. My family deserves to have their family and medical history. I went through 30 years of not knowing where I came from; the time has come to find out.

Searching for My Birth Mother

It is 1990 and before the Internet. There were computers but no AOL connection. It was a time when most people had landlines and cell phones were only had by the minority of wealthy people. Most were car phones with connected wires. Technology had not been invented yet. So, I made an appointment with Catholic Charities, the organization through which my parents adopted me.

I went to the appointment in Vineland, NJ, and spoke to a nun. I explained my story and told her I needed to gain my medical history and would appreciate her giving me my birth mother's name. She was polite but steadfast on the rules. She could not give me my birth mother's name. She told me that my birth mother was not from NJ and that she was a Catholic Irish gal and very young. I had that much information prior to arriving at her door. I left disappointed and upset. This is not going to be an easy feat. My next stop was to Woodbury, NJ, to make an appointment to see a judge to ask him to grant me my sealed records to be opened. The Clerk told me I had to write a letter explaining my request and she would call me after the judge had read my letter to see what the steps would be to open my records. Another bummer! I could be waiting a long time.

To my surprise, less than a week later, I received a call from the clerk. She scheduled an appointment with Judge Lindsey in the Woodbury, NJ court house. I arrived early on a Friday morning and was escorted into a small room off the courtroom. When Judge Lindsey entered the room, he handed me a tablet and pen and said, "I am going to give you the information you need, and I want you to write it down because I cannot give you the documents because they are sealed and belong to the courts."

I was dumbfounded as I thought I would be facing a court hearing, or at least a battle convincing the Judge why I needed these records. Judge Lindsey got right to the point and began giving me all the details of my birth mother. Starting with her name, her age at the time of my birth, and the state that she resided in when she relinquished me to Catholic Charities. There was no name listed for my birth father, but only that she was married when I was born. The Judge gave me her husband's last name and my birth mother's maiden name. So, after about 15 minutes of time, I had enough information to begin an accurate search. The Judge wished me good luck and hoped my son and I would soon be free of health problems. I thanked him for his help and support and was so grateful for his kindness.

My ride home was full of excitement and anticipation; I just may be able to find the lady who brought me into this world and, with any luck, gain all the medical records that I so desperately needed. My husband was going to help me, and the search was on! The first step was to order a Missouri phone book through NJ Bell. I never knew you could order a phone book from another state, but after calling 411 a number of times, I was told by the operator to order a phone book.

Back in 1991, there was free operator assistance offered to get phone numbers. Today, we have the internet; however, to get valid phone numbers, you have to pay for the service. I was able to order a free Missouri phone book, which would help us to find my birth mother. During this time, I was developing another problem. This problem was with our neighbors next door. Apparently, they were not happy that I was operating a childcare center next door to them. The woman began videotaping the children in the playground and calling the NJ State Licensing Bureau constantly and telling them I had too many children. Being unaware that my own children did not count in the number of children I was able to have in my facility, she was making phone calls and false reports to the State. I was getting unannounced visits from State-Licensing to count the children in my care.

It was not only annoying to me, but the State of NJ was becoming very annoyed at the frequent visits they had to endure. Thank God my inspector was friendly and understanding; after a few months, my neighbor's endless calls were ignored. But, the videotaping continued and a feud erupted to the point where she began to harass my customers. It was not a good situation for anyone. In the meantime, my phone book arrived and we began calling numerous Murphy's from the phone book. There were hundreds, but we would call every one of them if necessary.

I believe it was on a Sunday afternoon when my husband called John Kemp. He had the idea that we should start searching for my birth mother's maiden name rather than her married name. He went through his usual spiel about how his wife was sick, and he was looking for her birth mother, a memorized lingo that he repeated at least 25-30 times from prior calls. He wanted to know if he was related to Mary Murphy. John Kemp was the answer to all my prayers!!! He explained that he had a sister, Mary Murphy, who lived in St Louis, Missouri, and she had a bunch of kids. He then said that he hadn't seen her in years because they were estranged. He then told my husband of the reason why they were not close. The story was that their mother abandoned them when his sister was 7 and he was 4. He was adopted, and she went into foster care.

Oh my! A story that made me sad; if, indeed, John's sister was my birth mother, she grew up in foster care. He said if we gave him a few days, he would try and get us a phone number. Harry gave him our phone number, and he would call us back in a few days. After a few days of feeling as if I were sitting on pins and needles, the phone rang at 7:00 PM on a Wednesday.

Luckily, my husband answered the phone. I think he knew who it was upon seeing a Missouri phone number on our caller ID. John Kemp, who kept his birth name even after his adoption, was a blessing to me! He rattled off a phone number that he was told was his sister's phone number. He never said how he got the number but asked us not to tell his sister that he gave it to us. My husband thanked him and assured him he would not divulge how he got her unlisted phone number. I wanted to call immediately, but we had an end-of-the-school-year awards ceremony to attend at our daughter's school, so the phone call would have to wait. The very next day was filled with anxiety and anticipation because my husband was going to make the phone call to the lady who just might be my birth mother. I was too nervous to do it myself, therefore I had to wait until my husband got home from work. I knew this call could be the beginning of something wonderful, or it could be another disappointment if we learned we had the wrong lady, or worse, she was not receptive to our intrusion into her life. It could go either way, so my anxiety was building as the day grew later.

Finally, my last child was picked up from my childcare center, and my husband was home. We ordered a pizza for dinner, and after bathing my children and getting them in bed, the dreaded but hopeful call was made. He dialed the number and put the call on speaker so that I could listen. June 6, 1991, at 8:00 PM, The conversation went like this: Harry- "Hello, is this Mary Murphy"?

Mary- "Who wants to know"?

Harry- "You don't know me, but I'm calling you from NJ."

Mary- "Listen, if you are looking for money, I don't have any"!

Harry- "My name is Harry, and I need to know if you were in NJ in 1959"?

Mary- "Who is this"?

Harry- "My wife is sick, and we are looking for her birth mother. Did you have a baby girl in December of 1959 that you gave up for adoption"?

S I L E N C E......

Harry- "Hello"

Mary- "Yes, you have the right person, but I was raped, you know? You caught me off guard here, and I have my kids and grandkids here, and I rented a passenger van that is being packed to go to Georgia for my daughter's graduation, so I'm going to have to call you back."

Harry- "ok, no problem, can I give you my phone number"?

Mary-"Sure, let me get a pen; hold on a minute."

P A U S E.....

Mary-"ok, I'm ready"

Harry- rattles off our phone number

Mary- ok, Thank you, and listen, I apologize for being short with you because my ex-husband passed away, and I've been getting calls from collection agencies about unpaid debt, so I assumed you were a collector."

Harry- "I understand, so when can I expect to hear from you"?

Mary- "In about 3-4 days, after I return, will that be ok? If I may ask, how is your wife? Is it serious "?

Harry- "She has an illness that the doctors cannot diagnose."

Mary- "Well, please tell her I will keep her in my prayers; what is her name"?

Harry- "Dana"

Mary-"ok, Harry, thanks for calling, and I will call soon."

Harry- "Ok, have a safe trip."

Mary-"Thank you, talk soon. ByeBye"

Wow! That is all I could say about the call. We found my birth mother, but she did not sound like a nice person from my first impression. She acted standoffish and a bit nasty, to say the least.

My husband said, well, in her defense, she was probably in shock. I do not think she expected to hear from you after 31 years, and she had a houseful of family there that may or may not know about you. Well, maybe you are right, but I wouldn't act like that if I were in her shoes. So now I wait again!

The Truth Hurts

Sometimes, not knowing allows you the opportunity to believe things were the way your mind has conjured them to be. The fairytale story that I grew up believing that my favorite aunt, who bought me more gifts than Santa at Christmas, took me shopping, and treated me like a princess, was not my birth mother. This was hard to learn especially since my real beginning started through an awful offensive crime.

As I thought about the reality of my situation, I also began to feel sorry for my birth mother. Although it saddens me to learn how I was conceived, it gave me compassion for the lady who brought me into this world. I knew in 1959 that abortion was illegal, but so was marijuana, and that didn't stop people from smoking it. I am certain underground abortions were happening during my birth mother's pregnancy with me, and I felt thankful she opted to give me life. While waiting for her call, I resolved to stay positive and set aside my initial impressions until I knew more. Just as she'd promised, the phone rang on a Tuesday afternoon, but I missed it while I was busy settling the children down for their naps. After listening to the voicemail, I learned it was my birth mother, and she left a very pleasant message. Her voice was very sweet and not at all as she sounded the night Harry contacted her. She mentioned that if Dana had any questions for me, I should have her call. She left her phone number once more and said she looked forward to hearing from me.

So, I called her back. As my fingers pushed the 10 numbers needed to connect to this lady, I noticed my hands were shaking! I spoke to her for about an hour, listening to every word of her story and how I came to be. She told me a very detailed story. I hung up knowing I had 1 older sister, Sheila, who was 15 months older than me, and a younger sister, Susan, who was 9 years younger than me. She also told me I had two brothers, Keith, who was about 4 years younger than me, and Paul, who was 6 years younger than me. So, the lineup was supposedly Sheila, me, Keith, Paul and Sue.

However, there is a surprise to the lineup that I will share later. I told her about my medical issues, and she informed me that she, too, had a few pneumothoraxes, but she was told they were caused by embolisms in her lung. Could this be my problem? Wow! Embolisms could kill!!!! She talked about coming to NJ to meet me but had to find a traveling partner to come with her. She also explained that Sheila lived in Georgia and she was the one that just graduated from college; she asked me if I'd be willing to talk to Sheila because she wanted to talk to me.

I would be happy to talk to my sister, and, yes, tell her to call me. The conversation could have gone on for hours, but the children were waking up from napping, and I had to get back to work. We hung up with the idea that we would keep in touch. So, I now know my birthmother's name is MaryLou Murphy; she was 18 years old when I was conceived and 19 years old when I was born. She lived in St. Louis, Missouri, her entire life, except when her husband, who was in the Army, was stationed in Fort Monmouth, NJ.

Mary told me when her husband was shipped overseas to Iceland, she went back to St. Louis, with Sheila, and she told me that is where I was conceived. She also explained how it happened. The saga goes on.

Mary's Story

Mary was the first born to Andrew Kemp and Laura Shaw Kemp on June 8, 1941. She would have 1 brother, John Kemp, who was born in 1944. Apparently, Laura Shaw Kemp ran off to California with a gentleman friend and left Mary and John with her mother, Golda Kemp, with intentions to return home after two weeks. Well, Laura never came back, and Golda could not afford to care for Mary and John. So, John went into a home with a family; however, Mary went into an orphanage where she would spend 5 years being cared for by the nuns who operated the facility. When Mary was 12 years old, she learned that her mother was back in the area, so after school, one day, she decided to walk to her mother's home and knock on the door. Her mother had divorced her father and remarried a man named George Jovanovic

and had 3 more children with him. Gwen, Rose, and Larry were Mary's half-siblings. Mary moved back in with her mother at 12 years of age and became the built-in babysitter for her 3 younger siblings. Mary did not have a good childhood; spending 5 years in an orphanage was rough enough, but living with her mother and her alcoholic stepfather was no picnic either. Her mother would once again divorce and remarry a third husband, Kenneth Hart, who would give Mary another half-sister, Terri. At age 16, Mary would run off to Illinois and marry James Murphy, also 16, and was enlisted in the Army. They would move to NJ, where James was stationed at Fort Monmouth. On August 20, 1958, Mary gave birth to her first child, Sheila Lynn, born in Patterson, NJ Military Hospital. They would bring Sheila home to a second-floor apartment in the Highlands located in Monmouth County, NJ.

Not long after Sheila's birth, James would be stationed overseas in Iceland, and Mary went back to St. Louis, Missouri, where she would share a flat with a girlfriend. They would go out dancing and living life the best that they could. After a night out, they would return to their flat, where her girlfriend's friend would climb through a transom window and enter Mary's room. As

Sheila slept in a crib at the foot of Mary's bed, this man took advantage of Mary.

Sheila was just 6 months old when I was conceived. The pregnancy would send Mary back to NJ, where she would contact Catholic Charities for assistance in placing me for adoption. She was put in an apartment in Camden, NJ, and on December 17, 1959, she would give birth to me at Lady of Lourdes Hospital. She would christen me at the hospital with the name "Theresa Ann Murphy." Had my name been Smith or Brown, I wonder if my life would have been different. Since Mary was legally married, her husband would become my legal father, regardless of the fact that he was not my biological father. This posed a problem because James Murphy was in Iceland, and until he could return to New Jersey to sign the adoption papers, my adoption couldn't proceed.

I'm not sure where I spent the first three months of my life, but it seems I was in foster care, waiting for James Murphy to come back and relinquish his rights as my legal father. I do know I was christened a second time at St Theresa's Church in Runnemede, NJ before my parents adopted me in March of 1960. As the saying goes, the 3rd time is a charm because my parents would Christen me a third time as "Dana Marie" in April of 1960. I do believe I was the holiest baby ever born. Perhaps that continued through my life because, through all my ups and downs and twists and turns, I always felt that God was riding my bumper, making certain I made all the right turns. There may have been a few U-turns, but my faith was always there.

Mary Murphy -Birth Mother

Sisterly Love

A few days after speaking to my birthmother, Mary, I received a call from my sister, Sheila. She and I hit it off immediately! We talked for quite a while, and we discovered we had more in common than genetics. She was so easy to talk to and so sweet. She told me about her children, she had three girls, Jessica, Jennifer, and Janelle. She was also married and divorced and thinking about leaving her 2nd husband and moving back to St Louis, Missouri. She told me her oldest two girls were from her 1st husband, and Janelle was from her 2nd husband. She shared stories about her childhood, explaining how she took care of her younger siblings while her mother worked. She told me that her parents divorced when she was 12, and her father later remarried a woman named Bonna. She also mentioned that her father passed away in 1984, which meant I would never have the chance to meet the man who was my legal father at birth.

But the main surprise came when she began talking about Scott, and that he had delayed speech also. Perhaps it's a genetic thing. Being a bit confused, I asked Sheila who is Scott? With a slight giggle, she says well, he is actually James Scott, but we called him Scott because my Dad was James. Again, even more confused, I said well, who is James Scott? She replied.... "your brother, silly." My brother? Well, I was told I had 2 sisters and 2 brothers! What's the deal? Who is this Scott who was not in the lineup?

Well, you can imagine my dismay when she told me that Scott was born in August of 1961, making him 15 months younger than me. He was Mary's oldest son and named after his father. Wow!!!! So now I learn that I was one of 6 children, not 5! I had a sister 15 months older than me and a brother 15 months younger. Why was I not told about Scott? Why would my birthmother not divulge Scott? Sheila gave me the answer; she told me that when Scott was 16 years old, he was dared by one of his younger brothers and a friend to go into a convenience store with a cap gun under his coat and rob a store. He then escaped during a transfer to court and was a wanted teenager.

What!!!! I couldn't believe it; I was shocked, to say the least. I had a half-brother in prison! That's why his identity was kept from me. Had he not fled, he might have received probation or community service, but after being on the run for two years, he faced the full consequences of the law. He was caught and arrested in Georgia in 1980 and sentenced to 25 years! Again, I thought to myself, sometimes not knowing is better.

What am I going to learn next? I never said anything to Mary the next time I heard from her; I didn't want to cause problems in a family I was newly involved. I was grateful to know that at least Sheila was honest, and I knew we would become great friends. I would just bite my tongue and wait until Mary was ready to tell me about Scott. However, it bothered me that after telling Mary about my son's problems, she did not tell me about Scott, especially since he had delayed speech and some concerns. It may have a genetic link since Scott was her third child and first son. Harry Jr. Was my 3rd child and first son also.

Face to Face

It was the second week in August when I would meet my birth mother and her sister, Rose. They were coming to NJ. It would be a long drive by car from St. Louis, Missouri. Being planned for over a month, I was able to give my customers notice that I would be taking my vacation for the week she would be in town. The excitement was building. The plan would be that she would call me when they found a hotel/motel and were settled in. I would then drive to her motel.

I received a call that she was at Woodbury Police Department because she and Rose were involved in a car accident at the intersection of Tanyard Rd and Evergreen Ave in Woodbury, NJ. Apparently, a young guy ran the red light on Evergreen Ave and hit the front left corner panel of Mary's Honda Civic. Because she was out of state, she went to the Police Department to get an accident report for her insurance company. She would call me as soon as she could find a place to stay and get settled. What a way to begin this journey.

Around 7 PM, I got the call that she was at the Holiday Inn on Rt 130 in Brooklawn, NJ. She gave me her room number, and I headed out right away. It would take me about 20 minutes to arrive, and as I pulled up to the motel, I said a little prayer that this would be a positive meeting and that everything would go smoothly. I have to admit that I was actually more than nervous; I was truly scared of what could be. I never saw any pictures of her, so I had no idea what she looked like.

In 1991 there were no computers, no chat rooms, no Facebook! I was walking into a motel room blinded, with absolutely no idea what I would find. Would I meet a woman who I looked like? Or would she look at me as a bad memory in her life? As I got out of my minivan, the lump in my throat grew bigger, like I had swallowed a plum whole. I walked up to the door and knocked gently. Mary answered the door with a smile and hugged me. As I sat down on the bed, she introduced me to her sister, Rose, who was also very friendly and said, nice to meet the niece I never knew. I laughed and said, yes, it's been 31 years coming. We talked for a few hours and enjoyed a couple of beers, and I told them that this hotel was not located in the best neighborhood. They both agreed, asking me where they could go. I suggested the Dutch Inn in Gibbstown, NJ, as that would be safer and closer to where I lived.

So, it was settled that the next morning, after they checked out, they would go to the Dutch Inn, and I could come there and we would have dinner at the Hotel. Rose kept saying how much I looked like Mary and how much our mannerisms were the same. She said we even sat the same way. Mary agreed and said yes, without a doubt, you are definitely my daughter. So, I finally began to realize that finding my birthmother was a good thing to do. So, as I was getting ready to leave, I hugged them both goodbye and told them I'd see them tomorrow. Mary said it was a pleasure meeting me and looked forward to tomorrow. I knew they were both tired and needed to sleep. So, as I walked out the door and got into my van, I said to myself... You did it! You met the woman who brought you into this world!

The Dutch Inn

In 1991, the Dutch Inn was beautiful! The banquet room was decorated in a pretty French blue and gold decor, with stunning crystal chandeliers aligning the entire ceiling. Beautiful antique furniture and white tablecloths adorned every table. Truly Elegance at its finest. The hotel rooms offered an earlier time element, with big beautiful beds, cherry furniture, and all the bells and whistles that made this a beautiful piece of history. This was a place that Mary and Rose would remember with fond memories of a South Jersey Hotel in a quiet neighborhood in Gibbstown, NJ, A beautiful atmosphere to enjoy while spending time with me, the daughter she gave birth to 31 years ago. The evening was magical; we dined at the hotel restaurant, listened to a band, had a few drinks, and talked endlessly.

Eventually, Mary opened up about my brother Scott and explained why she had hesitated to mention him during our first conversation. She confessed that she thought that I would think less of her if I knew I had a brother in prison, and she didn't want to take that chance of losing the ability to have a relationship with me. I thanked her for telling me, and I explained to her how important honesty was to me. I have spent 31 years not having facts about my birth or where I came from, and I needed to know only truths, as I lived long enough with fantasies. She then told me about my father, his name was Larry. I began laughing hysterically, and with a perplexed look on Mary's face, she asked me what was so funny. When I caught my breath, I began to explain. "My first husband's name was Gary, my current husband's name is Harry, and now you tell me my birth father's name is Larry?"

"OMG!! Only in my world would this occur"! She and Rose started laughing along. It was funny, as who can say they had a Gary, Harry, and Larry in their life? It's really a remarkable rhyming story. We talked the night away, and I didn't leave to go home until 2:30 in the morning. I pulled out of the Dutch Inn parking lot and took a wrong turn; I was lost and had very little gas in my van and no damn idea where the hell I was! I can recall it being a dark road and no street lights no gas stations; and of course, this was before cell phones, so if I ran out of gas, I had no way of calling for help. I was praying and in tears. I can remember coming to a blinker light intersection with some tractor store on the corner. All I knew was wherever I was, I'd never been before! I turned around and followed the road back till I once again came upon an area close to the Dutch Inn; I found a gas station and thanked God! This was another one of those times that God was riding on my bumper. I finally made it home at 4:00 AM. Mary and Rose were coming to my house to meet my husband and children later today. Hopefully, their sense of direction is better than mine.

Thankful that I didn't hear from Mary until 1:00 PM, as I didn't wake until after 11:00 AM, which, with my daily routine, was very late! Having to get up every morning at 5:45 AM to open my center by 6:30 AM and sleeping until 11:00 was extremely late! I decided on Spaghetti and meatballs for dinner. I told Mary to come about 5:00 PM, so I could get the house cleaned up and have dinner ready before they arrived. Today, Mary and Rose would meet my family. My husband answered the door, and when I heard that Missouri accent talking, I came in from the kitchen to welcome them. They admired our home but were especially impressed with my daycare, which was decorated with a Sesame Street Theme. Big Bird and Cookie Monster, Bert and Ernie, they couldn't believe how cute it was. We ate dinner, and both Mary and Rose were busy chatting with my children.

Kristin was 10 and was filled with questions. Erin was 7 and was busy entertaining them with her dancing and singing. Harry Jr. was 2 but still not verbal. Mary commented on how much Kristin looked like us. She told me Harry did remind her a bit like Scott as a baby, but that she thought Harry also looked like us. I told her that Erin looked just like her dad but did have more of my personality traits than Kristin. It's funny how my oldest daughter looked like me but acted more like her father, and Erin looked like her dad but acted more like me. Who will ever understand genetics? Rose chimed in with the comment that Mary had 5 children she raised, and the one she gave away looked most like her! Even my husband agreed that I looked very much like Mary. It was a delightful evening, and everyone enjoyed themselves. I hated to see it end, especially knowing that Mary and Rose would be leaving the next day. I felt a bit down as I said goodbye, but we talked about planning a trip to St. Louis in the future so I could meet my brothers and sisters. That would be next on the agenda.

The Blended Family

As one may know, the blended family has its problems. I had 2 daughters from my ex-husband, and Harry had 1 daughter from a previous relationship. Before we married, he was not seeing his daughter at all. I convinced him that he should develop a relationship with his daughter right after we married. Back then, his daughter Laurel was 2 months older than my daughter Erin; both girls were 4 at the time. We went to a lawyer to arrange visitation with his daughter. It was arranged, and he would be getting his daughter 1 weekend a month. I went out and bought all 3 girls a matching Christmas dress, and we took all 4 children to see Santa Claus and have a family portrait taken. In the beginning, all was wonderful, and then things went south. His daughter's mother was not happy with Laurel having a relationship with my family. Especially me! She was making things so difficult that it was making an impossible situation for everyone, including her own daughter.

One day, when we went to pick up Laurel at her grandmother's house, where she and her mother lived. The grandmother reached through the open passenger window, where I was sitting, and punched me in the side of my jaw! For absolutely NO reason, just because she felt like it. Well, my husband was furious! After Laurel was buckled in her seatbelt, he backed out of the driveway and went directly to the Clayton Police Station. He had an officer come outside to the van to look at my face. He filed charges, and as you guessed, this caused a war! Court Hearings that were downright ugly, false accusations against me, and then came a time Laurel's Mother was chasing me through Oak Valley and down Rt. 45, where she actually caused my van to slide into a guardrail. I believe this was enough for me! Visitations would no longer include me or my children!

Harry tried having visitations alone with his daughter for a brief time, but when Laurel began trying to include her mother in these excursions, that was the end of it. Harry continued paying his child support through the courts but had no ties to his daughter. It was a sad situation for years, and up until Laurel turned 18 years old, her mother would take Harry back to court for more child support over and over again. We had legal fees galore, and because Harry was often out of work due to his line of work, the legal fees, as well as the child support, fell on my shoulders to pay. The two people that were hurt the most through this ordeal were my husband and his daughter. It is really a shame that his daughter's mother took away the chance for her daughter to have a relationship with her father.

The Trip to St. Louis

There have been numerous phone calls between my birth mother and myself since our first meeting in August. I also had many conversations with my sister, Sheila. I wanted to meet the rest of my siblings and Mary's boyfriend, Ron, who she lived with. Sheila had left her husband in Georgia and moved back to St Louis with her 3 girls. I never spoke to my brothers or my other sister, and I was anxious to meet the rest of the gang. Since I closed my center from December 24th until January 2nd every year for the Christmas Holiday, we decided that we would go to St. Louis over that week. We would spend Christmas Day at home with our family and leave Christmas night.

We had Christmas dinner with our parents; all would come to our house and then clean up and ship out. We left our house at 10:00 PM to start the journey. We thought it would be easier to travel at night with 3 children. They could sleep, and we would take turns driving. I recall stopping in Maryland for a bathroom run and purchasing coffee to keep us awake. When it was my turn to drive, I recall being somewhere with a lot of mountains on both sides and twisting and turning around sharp bends. I think I was in Virginia, but I can tell you that it was a bit challenging navigating through the area, especially being sleep-deprived.

After about 3 hours, I pulled into a rest stop and woke Harry. I needed to use the bathroom, I needed food and coffee, and I needed him to drive. It was dawn, and the sun was beginning to rise. We had hours more to drive, and I needed to recharge. The children were still sacked out in the back of the van. We stopped for about 15 minutes. We were surprised at how well-behaved our children have been thus far. After fueling up, we got back on the highway. Within 15 minutes, we hear a small voice," Are we there yet"? Then another small voice, "I have to go to the bathroom," and then it begins! Harry Jr. was up and he was irritable because he didn't get enough sleep.

We continued to drive down the highway, looking for an exit or rest stop. Then there it was: the "Golden Arches" appeared, so we got off i-70 and took our children to McDonald's. Pancakes and sausage times 3, 1 milk, 1 chocolate milk, 1 orange juice, 2 egg McMuffins, and two coffees for us. Back in 1991, bathrooms usually did not offer changing tables for babies, so I would be changing Harry Jr on the back seat of our van. On the road again, we traveled through Ohio, and somewhere in Indiana, we stopped again.

By the time we hit the Arch in St Louis, it was dark and about 8:00 PM, and of course, we got lost! Although I had Mary's address, there was no GPS, and we had no cell phones. After driving 30 minutes, Harry stopped at a gas station for directions; we had driven 20 miles in the wrong direction and had to turn around. After driving for about an hour, we stopped at a 711, and I called Mary from a pay phone. She knew exactly where we were and came to get us. We followed her back to her house, which was basically only 3 minutes away. She lived on a dead-end street, and her house was a cute little white stucco house that resembled a cottage you would see on Christmas cards. She had a white picket fence, and there was a porch with an old church pew that set across the front window. Quaint but cute.

Upon entering the front door, I was greeted by her tiny white poodle and a basset hound that followed behind. The house was decorated for the Holidays, and her furniture was full of beautiful antiques. There was a fire lit in the fireplace, with a beautiful antique etched mirror above. The Dining room had a chestnut wood table with benches. Her kitchen was small but very homey, equipped with a very old Hoosier. The home had two bedrooms and a bathroom. She took us downstairs, where she had a giant pit set, TV, and pool table. There were sliding glass doors that led to a backyard with an above-ground pool and deck. The walls downstairs were adorned with old metal signs that reminded me of The Cracker Barrel. She had set up a bed downstairs for the girls, and we would sleep upstairs in a bedroom that had a crib in it for Harry Jr.

We were starving because we hadn't eaten since 2:00 PM, and it was after 10:00 PM. Mary ordered a couple of pizzas, and we had pizza and a few beers before turning in for the night. Tomorrow, we would meet everyone else. I awoke the next morning to the smell of sweet coffee. I got up and left Harry sleeping. Mary and I sat in the Dining room, drinking coffee and chatting. Mary had lived with Ron for about 9 years but was not married. Ron had an appraisal business, and he also held a Real Estate Broker's License in 3 states. Mary went to school to receive her appraising license and worked for Ron. Mary explained that Sheila(sister) and Keith(brother) were going to school currently for appraising so they could soon work for Ron also. He ran his business from a commercial building. She would show it to me later. She would show it to me later.

Although Mary and Ron lived within city limits, the town was called Afton and actually didn't look like a city at all. The neighborhood looked a lot like NJ with the exception of all the hills. Missouri has huge mountains overlooking the highways. My brother Keith was the first to come to Mary's to meet me. He was a good-looking young man with dark brown hair and blue eyes. He was full of fun. I liked him immediately.

I learned that Keith was divorced and had two daughters, Kate (6) and Amber (4). He was currently dating a girl named Jennifer. He told me my brother Paul was also divorced and had 2 boys with his Ex-wife, Christopher (5) and Zachery (3), and that he was currently living with a girl named Kathy, and they had a son, Brennan (6 mos), Scott was still in prison and had been since age 17!

Susan had 1 son at age 16, Tony (4), but never married his father. She was living with a guy named Nick, and they had a son, Nicholas (2) Nick, who was also divorced and had his daughter, Rachel (7), living with them also. So, there it was, I too, divorced and remarried; I fit right into the equation. We were all going to Susan's later to meet her and her sons Tony and Nicholas and Nick and his daughter Rachel. Susan lived in a big cape cod on a busy highway. She met us at the door, hugged me, and offered us something to drink. She was pretty and very friendly. Her live-in boyfriend Nick was funny and very nice; he worked for Boeing and made a good salary.

The house was very big. All the kids were upstairs playing like Wild Indians, and Nick and Harry went to get a few cases of beer. The day ran into the night, and it was fun to hang out with Sue & Nick and Mary & Ron. Tomorrow we were going to a Pub in St Louis where everyone was coming. St. Louis was a pretty city, unlike Philadelphia, and all the people we have met here are so friendly. There is a totally different vibe in Missouri compared to NJ. Strangers on the street say hello and how are you? Being raised a Jersey girl, if a stranger would ask, "How are you"? We would ignore them and keep walking.

East Coast people are just not as friendly as Mid-Western people. So far, the trip has been fun; tonight, as we pulled up to the Pub, Keith was outside smoking a cigarette, and he told us they had a table. Now, growing up with one sister, I was not accustomed to being in such a large family group. Harry and I followed Mary and Ron into the Pub. We walked over to a table big enough to sit 20 people and half the table was full, I was introduced to Paul (brother) and his girlfriend Kathy. Paul, also good-looking and very tall, said, "Welcome, long-lost sister" "how the hell are you"? We hugged, and he introduced me to his girlfriend, Kathy. A cute, petite young girl, sweet as a button. Then Sheila, who I now learned they call Shel, came up and said, "Well, we finally meet, sister." We hugged. I could not believe how much She and I looked alike! She introduced me to Jennifer, who was Keith's girlfriend.

Sue and Nick yelled..." Hey, good to see you again!" and then there was also Rose and her husband, who drove up from Springfield, Missouri, and then Ron's two daughters, Dawn and Melissa, and their boyfriends. So, everyone was waiting to order food. This pub was famous for its chicken and ribs, so we all ate, drank, and were merry! I was very lucky to have everyone so receptive and welcoming towards my family and me. We planned a trip the next day to visit Grant's Farm, which Busch Brewing

Company owns. This farm was built by Ulysses S. Grant in 1840. Eventually bought by Busch Brewing Company, and is now a frequently visited amusement park filled with animals, and it offers buggy rides pulled by Clydesdale horses. Exhibits, stores in which to purchase souvenirs, Kiddie rides and tons of food.

It was a day I'll never forget! There were so many of us, with all the kids, there were 21 of us all together! Mary and Ron paid for all the tickets; I can't imagine what that bill was. The next day, Mary and Ron would take Harry and I and our children on a train ride to see St Louis Union Station; we would have lunch and walk around and see exhibits and bands playing music and walk through the stores. The kids loved the train ride the best! Another nice day. As our visit was soon coming to an end, Mary made dinner, and everyone came to her house for the last night of our visit. When I tell you that the children had to eat in shifts, I literally mean it. 14 children needed to eat, and 11 adults. That's like crazy! But it was nice to see everyone before we left. We would pack the van after everybody left and get up early to hit the road. Well, the alarm went off at 5:00 AM; we were collecting a few last-minute items when Mary came out to say Goodbye. As we opened the front door to leave we were stunned as the cold air and blowing snow hit us in the face! OMG! It was snowing, and this was going to be a trip from Hell to get home!

Driving through Hell

This was not going to be a pleasant trip. It had just started snowing, but the storm was coming from the East. This meant we would be driving right into the storm. The further East we drove, the worse the storm got! Needless to say, Harry would be driving the whole trip home. We made stops for gas and food, but basically, we drove non-stop. It took us 18 hours to drive from NJ to St. Louis, but it was going to take us a lot longer to get home. We passed vehicles broken down on i-70, as well as vehicles just pulled over to take a break from driving through the storm. The trip was so scary I swore I'd never make this trip again.

Then again, I swore I'd never have another child after my first, and there were 3 children in the back seat. The roads were getting so slippery that Harry was driving 40 miles an hour. We watched the sunrise and the sunset, yet we still were not home! I recall stopping in West Virginia at a rest stop at 7:00 PM, which meant we had been driving for 14 hours, and we were still at least 6.5 hours from home if we were driving on good roads in good weather. We couldn't even stop and stay in a hotel until the storm was over because I had to open my childcare center on Thursday, January 2nd, at 6:30 AM, and I had to get milk, food, and snacks for the children beforehand.

We needed to get home. I was not spending New Year's Eve on the road! So, after an hour at the rest stop to eat, use the restroom, and gasp, we were on the road again. The roads were so terrible that by the time we got to Pennsylvania, we had to stop! The snow was coming down so hard, and there were crashes all over the place. We stopped at a rest stop called Midway Service Center, where we would sit for a couple of hours. Harry was exhausted, and the stress was over the top from driving head-on through the nasty storm. After he slept an hour, we went into the rest stop and sat down and ate Roy Rogers Roast beef sandwiches and our children had chicken nuggets.

We ordered two large coffees to go, and by 12:30 AM, we were back on the road. Harry estimated we would be home by 5:00 AM. As you can imagine, he did not count on the stops for bathroom runs and our breakfast and coffee or for the backed-up toll booths from the mounting snow. Or for the fact that the roads were getting icier from the cold temperature. I was never as happy or relieved as after we drove over to The Walt Whitman Bridge and were back in NJ. Until you drive in a van through a snowstorm, with 3 children in tow, from Missouri to NJ for 25 hours, you will never fully understand the exuberant joy I felt when we pulled into our driveway at 6:16 in the morning. It was Home Sweet Home on Steroids!

Welcome in1992!

Time to celebrate; however, after sleeping barely 6 hours after returning home from our agonizing trip in a blizzard, the celebration was slim. Since the children slept through most of the drive, they were not tired, and at 11:30 AM, I was forced to rise and take care of my motherly duties. Harry Jr. was 3 years old and was full of energy. The girls were at the age where they could entertain themselves for a while, but Harry Jr. was a handful. He would sit on the floor and spin in circles when feeling anxious; he would kick holes in the walls when he was angry. He tested my patience at times, but I kept researching and reading, trying to help him in every way I could. I would not catch up on my lost sleep today because I had to get up and feed my children. I would be making a run to the grocery store to get items for the daycare children and find something to make for dinner. After all, it is New Year's Eve, and I wondered if I'd make it to midnight to ring in the new year.

Life is filled with ups and downs, but I always found a way to make it through the tough times. After a long trip from Missouri in a snowstorm, we made it home safely, and I now have an extended family that I know will be a blessing. It has been a very eventful year, and tonight, we will ring in the New Year. Well, the girls made it up to ring in the New Year- however, Little Harry was fast asleep, which made for a quiet and uneventful New Year. Which was just as well for hubby and me because we were cruising with very little gas left in our engines. The girls banged their pots on the front porch, and we watched as our neighbors lit up the sky with fireworks in celebration.

It's 1992 and as I toasted my husband, I wondered what will 1992 bring? Will our son start to talk this year? Will my daughters do well in school? Will my neighbor leave me alone, or will we have to move? I absolutely loved our home! I loved the area; I grew up in this town. This was home! I have a successful daycare, and for the most part we were happy. But we could be happier if my son started talking and developing equal to his age. He was falling further behind with every year. I still don't know why I'm sick and why I'm living with pain that was absolutely excruciating at times! After the hoopla was over and Dick Clark was done rocking in the New Year, we retired to our beds. My bed never felt so good as it did tonight. Before I closed my eyes to sleep, I prayed for 1992 to be a good year.

Kiddie Korral Expands!

In 1992, we decided to move the daycare out of our home. My waiting list was growing to heights I never dreamed would happen. We had already tried to turn our entire home into a licensed center. However, our neighbor put a stop to that when she showed up at the planning board meeting to object to our plan. There was no choice but to relocate the center. The situation had become unbearable, with our neighbor constantly videotaping the children attending my facility.

The escalating hostility was starting to affect our family life, creating a tension that felt like a modern-day Hatfields and McCoys feud. We ended up renting a building near the township municipal building. We had a lot of renovations to do to get approval through the State Licensing of NJ. My husband and I worked at night to get the building ready. On top of the stress from our neighbors, my son was still not speaking, and my mystery illness was peaking to the point that I was being rushed to the hospital on a monthly basis, suffering from severe pain caused by pneumothorax!

By the time we rang in the New Year of 1993, we still had 3 months left of work to do to my new building, and it is safe to say that 1992 did not prove to be a good year, so we welcomed 1993 with open arms anticipating a better year!

The year of our Miracle

We continued working at night on the building that would soon be the new "Kiddie Korral," and our kids returned to school; the holidays were over, and we went back to the grind of working day and night. My husband was working for a local contractor by day and working on my center at night. I was working in my daycare all day from 6:30 AM till 6:00 PM, and on occasion, when my mother could come to watch our kids, I'd help him at the new facility at night. We were exhausted and wondered if we would ever get it done. The girls were doing wonderful in school, but our son was another story. When we met with his teachers to discuss his IEP (individual education plan), we were told he would have to attend a school in Haddonfield, NJ, the following school year. This school was for deaf children, and although he could hear, he wasn't speaking, so he would have to learn sign language so he could communicate.

As I sat and listened to the plan for my son, the tears rolled down my cheeks. I went home with a heavy heart, and I prayed for a miracle. In February I decided to take him to church with me one Sunday. It was the Feast of St. Blaise, the church would be blessing throats after mass, and I was having Harry's throat blessed! I had faith in the power of prayer and in God to help him.

This occurred on February 7th, 1993; I knew the school would start testing in April. If a miracle was going to happen, it had to be soon. It had to be now! It was two weeks later when he spoke his first word, he said mine! He picked up a toy and said mine. I couldn't believe it. I cried tears of joy, and within a week later, he was putting words together to make sentences. The teachers were amazed, and I was filled with happiness beyond bliss. My Lord has blessed him with a miracle that I will be forever grateful for. Harry took the kindergarten test in April and passed with flying colors! My oldest daughter Kristin and her friend Erica decided they were entering a pageant for "Little Miss Mantua," and of course, my younger daughter Erin said she wanted to do it, too.

So we went shopping for two pretty dresses that my daughters picked out for themselves, and both girls were competing for the title of Little Miss Mantua. It was a small-town pageant held at J. Mason Tomlin School. There were about 30-35 contestants, and most of the girls were in 5th and 6th grade. My daughter Erin was one of the youngest contestants, but she was a. Shining Star! She rose to the occasion like she was born to be on stage! Erin Marie, at age 9, became Little Miss Mantua in 1993! She rode on top of a convertible Mustang in the Mantua Twp Parade on Fun Day and made her mother proud. God is good, and with any luck, I would have my health restored, and my new school would soon open. Harry was going to go to Sewell School Elementary in September in a regular kindergarten class. No school for the deaf, no special class, regular kindergarten, and he was going to be fine. Hallelujah!

Next came all my inspections for my new daycare and preschool. First the township and then the State of NJ. It was a long haul, but finally, in June of 1993, I received all COs and my new license to operate my school at 471 Main St in Mantua, NJ. I now had a license for 39 children. Life is good! God is Great!! I interviewed about 5 teachers to join my staff, Barbara Sheila and myself. I hired Miss Judy as my Head Teacher, and she is the lady who officially changed my facility from a childcare center to an official preschool. She was a magnificent teacher and I pride a lot of my success to her. But I also have to send kudos out to Miss Barbara and my beloved MomMom Sheila! We were the starting staff of Kiddie Korral, and I will be forever grateful to these two special ladies also. Needless to say, "The Kiddie Korral" opened, and my enrollment was filled in less than one month! 1993 was a fantastic year!

The Axe Drops

It's like I said before, when all is going great the axe will drop! It was a crisp autumn evening, and we decided to take our kids to Wendy's for dinner after work. Back in 1993, Wendy's had a great salad bar that we liked, and the kids loved Wendy's chicken nuggets. I had just started eating my salad when I decided to use the ladies ' restroom. I can recall locking the door and getting a sharp pain in my chest. I do not recall falling to the floor, nor can I tell you how long I laid on the floor. The next thing I remember is the manager of Wendy's and 3 paramedics lifting me to a stretcher and taking me to Underwood Hospital in Woodbury, NJ. It wasn't till I saw a doctor who informed me that my husband and children were banging on the door, and I wasn't responding. The manager unlocked the door and called an ambulance. It was determined that I suffered another pneumothorax, probably fell, hit my head, and knocked myself out. I spent two days in the hospital with another chest tube! This was getting to be a real problem!

After being released, I was referred to an endocrinologist and a pulmonary doctor. Neither could help me! I was being told I had blebs (which everyone with lungs has) that were popping by one doctor, which was causing my pneumothorax. Another doctor in the hospital told my husband I had a mental problem, and my mind was making my lungs collapse! I continued to see one doctor after another, searching for an answer. I went to numerous hospitals every month with a pneumothorax, thinking that someone had got to know why my right lung kept collapsing. I went to Underwood, JFK, Dupont, University of Penn, Jefferson in Philadelphia, and Temple Hospital, and none of them could help me. I was feeling lost and had exhausted all avenues for the mystery to be solved.

I had a preschool to run and 3 children to care for; I was losing weight and sick all the time! I kept being diagnosed with pleurisy and or pneumonia every month. I was so overwhelmed and becoming angrier by the day. I was becoming, in no lesser words...." a miserable bitch"! I needed the pain to stop so that I could live my life. Perhaps God could give me one more miracle. I'd pray every night, and yet I still continued to suffer. I didn't know where to turn, I had done all I could do to help myself. I thought finding my birth mother would be the answer; I thought traveling to different hospitals and doctors would be my remedy, but it was all in vain.

In February of 1994, Wenonah Medical hired a new doctor for their staff. Dr Jeffrey Alken was the new doctor. So, of course, I made an appointment with him. He was very handsome and charming, but he had no clue what was wrong with me. He began sending me every month for a chest x-ray. I had so many chest X-rays I should be glowing! Every month, it was the same result: another pneumothorax, another chest tube! I'd be hooked up to an IV with morphine being pumped into my veins every single month! This had to stop! I needed help! I needed relief.

One Sunday afternoon I was watching a show called Medical Mysteries, and I wrote a letter to the show to have my story aired. After months of more pneumothoraxes and chest tubes, I still hadn't heard from the TV show, so I called ABC Network. I was desperate! I spoke to Anita Brickman, who did a health segment on channel 6 about unsolved medical problems. She was very interested in my story and told me to ask my family doctor if he would allow her to interview him. Dr. Jeffrey Alken agreed to go on the show with me.

In May 1994, Channel 6 visited my home with a crew and TV cameras to film my story. They also recorded a segment at my preschool. The entire feature aimed to help me find a diagnosis. I was being denied my medical bills to be paid by AmeriHealth Insurance because I had No Diagnosis! I had medical bills well over $20,000.00 and mounting daily. It was becoming a grave situation so I was praying that this health segment would bring me answers. To NO avail! In July 1994, Erin entered the Little Peach Pageant at the 4-H fair in Mullica Hill, NJ. Again, she came away with the crown and the title of "Little Miss Peach"! While Erin was making the newspapers for being a little Pageant Star, my oldest daughter was making her mark on the soccer fields. She was playing wing and was scoring more goals that she was becoming our soccer star! She would be entering HS in less than a week and trying out for the Clearview Soccer Team.

It was on Sunday afternoon during Labor Day weekend that I received a small margin of hope. My husband had taken our kids out shopping, and I was home alone; I was carrying a basket of laundry up from the basement where our laundry room was located. I think I was on the 5th step when the pain hit me again! I dropped the basket and watched the clothes tumble down the steps; hunching over, I grabbed the phone and called my mother to come to take me to the hospital. Underwood was the closest, so within 20 minutes, I was back in the emergency room. A doctor, on furlough from Chile, saw me. He asked me if I had my period. At first, I thought, why are you asking me this? I was not willing to have a gynecological examination, so I wondered why he was asking. I said I didn't have my period, but it was due in about 4-5 days. The next words he would say, even in broken English, were music to my ears!

He said I may have systemic endometriosis and that this could be what was causing my pneumothoraxes. I said how can I fix this? He said I'd have to have surgery to tell for sure. He ordered another chest x-ray, and no doubt I had another pneumothorax. So, another chest tube and more morphine. All the doctors on staff disagreed with the Dr. from Chile; I was told it was very, very rare and doubted that this was the cause. After leaving the hospital, I began researching on my computer, and I was certain that I definitely had systemic endometriosis. I told my family doctor and he was skeptical also. I made an appointment with a new endocrinologist from Jefferson Hospital in Philadelphia, who listened to me and said he would try Lupron 7.5mg. Injections monthly to see if it helps.

When I was scheduled for my first shot, I was told my health insurance would not cover the shots without a diagnosis. Another brick wall! It was then it finally hit me, Murphy's Law curses me. How many more chest tubes can they shove through my ribs?

Complications Continue

I went to a Dr Lynch affiliated with Underwood Hospital, who told me that my gall bladder was the culprit of my pain. So, I was admitted to Underwood, where my gall bladder was removed. Two weeks later, I suffered another pneumothorax. I have now had my appendix and gall bladder removed, and still, the pain in my lung continues. Ever since the Dr. from Chile mentioned systemic endometriosis, I have been documenting my symptoms.

I can now say by the 14th day of my cycle, I begin feeling this pain that starts out as a dull pain and gets stronger by the 20th day. By the 22nd or 23rd day of my cycle, I get pain so excruciating that breathing becomes extremely painful, and this is usually when my lung collapses. I keep telling my family doctor (Jeffrey Alken) that I am positive I have systemic thoracic endometriosis. I explained to him that AmeriHealth Insurance was refusing to pay my medical bills, and I needed a diagnosis to go to the hospital. He writes me a script for Hydrocodone 5 mg. and tells me to take it only when I am in dire pain. So, I now see how this is going to be: just take oral pain meds and deal with this awful, excruciating pain every month!

Well, this was not going to work; the pain was so bad that 5 mg of hydrocodone didn't even touch the pain! I am pretty much ready to give up because living the way I am is not living! The only relief I get is 2 days after my period starts, which lasts for 10-12 days, and then it all starts up again. The stress of now knowing what is coming is causing havoc in my life. Imagine having to make all your plans within a 10-12 day a month schedule. Having to make a schedule for when you can vacation or make plans as simple as when you can be intimate with your husband. Knowing that every month for almost 71/2 years, you will spend at least 3 days in the hospital every month! The doctors look at you like you are from outer space, and they almost never sympathize with what you are going through. Living with the fear of dying every day. It sucks every day in every way!

At the beginning of December 1994, I had the worst pain I had ever experienced, and I didn't care if I was billed a million dollars; I was going to the hospital. I ended up in Underwood once again, having to deal with this arrogant Dr Lynch. I could barely breathe, and I was screaming in pain! I need this problem fixed! When the results of my x-ray came back this time, my lung was more than 55% collapsed, and they recommended surgery to see what was going on and do what needed to be done to fix me. I agreed to have the surgery.

After I awoke, I had another chest tube, and I was in so much pain that there were no words to explain. The Dr. told me they removed my pleura and stapled my lung to my chest wall. They also put talc powder in there to help adhere my lung to my rib cage. He told me that my pleura was covered with lesions so badly that there were too many to remove them all. I would have bled to death on the table. The lesions that were removed were sent to pathology to be biopsied, and with any luck, we would know what was wrong with me in a day or two.

In the meantime, I had stitches in my upper chest and staples inside my chest wall that would remain there forever! It hurt to breathe, and I had to stay propped up in the bed to drain the blood from my chest. Agony is putting it mildly. I spent my birthday, Christmas, and New Year's Eve and Day in the hospital! This was truly the longest hospital stay I ever experienced. The Dr was concerned that I might have cancer, so as I sat in the bed in dying pain, I prayed harder than I ever did before!

When the doctor stepped into my room very early on December 20th, two days after my surgery, he looked at me with a grim face and said I have your results. No one was there with me at 7:00 am to hold my hand or offer me support, and I was very nervous about what he was going to tell me. He said, "Looks like You were right." You have what we call systemic pulmonary endometriosis, and you had hundreds of what we call endometrial implants in your right pleura. We hope since the pleura was removed that, we were able to get the majority of the implants out, and perhaps you will be cured. However, I am 100% sure and guarantee that your right lung will no longer collapse because we put 150 staples in the chest wall to hold your lung affixed to your chest wall. Therefore, you should not suffer from any more pneumothoraxes. He told me I would have to remain in the hospital for two weeks at least until the blood had drained from my chest and we were sure the lung had healed. Well, I thanked him for helping me, and I praised the Lord! I would miss all the holidays with my family, but perhaps I will go home a healthy woman for the first time in over 7 years. The feeling of relief of finally knowing what medical mystery I had suffered with since 1989 was over! Or was it?

On January 2nd, 1996, a team of doctors entered my room to remove my chest tube; I was going home. Because this chest tube was inserted over two weeks ago, the scar tissue and flesh had wrapped around it to make taking it out the worst pain I ever felt! It took two doctors to pull it out, and it felt like my entire insides were coming out with it. I had to hold my breath while they literally yanked it out like they were playing tug of war! I would never wish this pain on my worst enemy; it was so bad that I couldn't even talk afterward. The tears came, but no sound. I just sat on the bed and wiped the tears off my face. The doctor was asking me questions, but all I could do was nod my head. It absolutely put me in momentarily frozen shock. I was told I might cough up a little blood for a day or two from removing the chest tube, but it was normal and nothing to worry about. I was given pain medicine to go home with. I made an appointment to see the doctor in his office two weeks later. The ride home was slow from snow covered roads. I had missed a big snow storm, as well as all the holidays with my family.

Moving to Great Heights

Recovery was moving quickly, and so was my business. I saw the Dr. and was released to go back to all normal activities. I returned to work. First on my agenda was to hire more employees. My enrollment was packed, and the waiting list was very long, with families waiting to enroll their children. It was the spring of 1996 when I hired Miss Chrissy, who would prove to be one of my most valuable employees. She started out as my toddler room teacher, but she would help me with office paperwork and anything and everything that I needed a hand.

By the summer of 1996, the school was so successful that my husband and I began talking about another expansion. In the childcare business, the amount of space you have is paramount to your success. The State of New Jersey required 35 square feet per child; therefore, the more space you had, the more children you could enroll. My waiting list became so long that I had as many children waiting as I had enrolled.

The biggest problem was summertime when families of enrolled children wanted to bring their school-age children to the school. It was then I came up with the idea to rent a space in Timberline Shopping Center and design a facility for school-aged children. This was going to be a challenge because I was one person and I would have to be running back and forth from Mantua to Sewell and divide my Director's time between the two. I would also have to retrofit a storefront into NJ State-Licensing qualifications to get a license to operate. All this was enough for anyone to be able to accomplish, but for someone who was not 100% healthy, it was going to be a tough nut to crack.

My husband was all for it, and said he would handle all the construction end of it. I agreed to do it, hiding the fact that the pain had returned to my lungs. It started in April, and every month, it grew worse. In July, I began getting pain in my left lung and, upon getting a chest x-ray, learned the endometriosis had spread to my left lung! I continued to ignore the pain and continued taking a pain pill when it got unbearable. Dr Alken sent me to a gynecologist who put me on a hormone called Danazol. It was a male hormone, which would hopefully stop the estrogen production, which would stop the endometriosis from growing. I decided since it spelled out my first name, it was made for me, so I would try it. I was given 450mg pills that I had to take 4 times per day. I was getting migraine headaches, and my face was breaking out terribly. My hair and skin were very oily, and my voice was getting deeper.

When I started seeing dark hair appearing around my upper lip, I was determined to stop the medicine; I certainly was not growing a mustache. The doctor decided to try a patch with only 5mg. of estrogen in it as an add-back therapy to reduce the side effects. So, the Dr called in the prescription, and I picked up 3 patches at the drugstore. I placed the patch on my hip as directed. Within 3 hours after placing the patch on my hip, I was in the Emergency room with severe pain. The chest x-ray showed that my left lung was beginning to deflate from the left middle side of my left lung. So, apparently, the implants were in the middle of this lung. So, they sent me home with pain meds and told me not to ever use the estrogen patch again!

What I discovered through the years I suffered with this disease was that, basically, my lungs were behaving like a uterus. When I was getting close to starting my period, my abdomen would swell, and I would get cramps. At the same time, the implants in my lungs would swell as well. As the implants got bigger over the months, they would cause a hole in my lung that would collapse my lung! But, what I also learned through trial and error was that once my hormone level dropped through menstruation, the implants would shrink, and my lung would stop hurting and inflate itself without a chest tube. Knowing this, I was determined that after having 41 chest tubes inserted in my right lung, I would not have 41 chest tubes put in my left lung! I would persevere through this pain with the help of pain medication.

(In 2002, I went back to the endocrinologist at Jefferson Hospital in Philadelphia and began the Lupron 7.5 injections. The Lupron7.5 injections are a drug called (leuprolide acetate) it is a man-made form of gonadotropin-releasing hormone (GnRH) that is used for men to treat prostate cancer and used for women to treat symptoms of endometriosis (which is an overgrowth of uterine lining outside of the uterus). This drug was approved by the FDA to be used for 3 months and no longer than 6 months. I was on this drug for 14 months!

The drug works to shut down a person's pituitary gland, which depletes the body of all hormones. The side effects are horrendous, but in my case, the alternatives were few. I didn't want to have a hysterectomy at 39 years of age. After agreeing to the treatment, I received my first shot. It was delivered by a needle 5 inches long and jabbed into my hip muscle. I realized within days that I was becoming the worst version of myself. I was happy, sad, hot, cold, sleepless, tired, and the most miserable bitch with a capital B! My mood swings were off the chart! I think I experienced every morbid side effect from this drug. 14 months later, I had no period! No lung pain, but instead, I traded for vision problems, balance problems, dizziness, hot flashes, chills, joint pain, nausea, constipation, and no sex drive at all! I went into instantaneous menopause. It was a hard time, yet somehow, through the Grace of God. I survived!)

During my treatment with Danazol, the next-door neighbor became more than I cared to deal with. So, in April of 1997, we sold our house and moved into a Big, Beautiful Home in a development around the corner called Rosewood. The house was originally the sample home for the development. We purchased the home from a man who had recently lost his wife. We got a good deal for this beautiful brick-front colonial. It absolutely had everything we wanted.

However, the biggest feat was that I was able to open my second location, "Kiddie Korral for the Big Kids." It was the end unit of a strip mall, with a wooded, grassy area across the parking lot, which allowed me to install a playground for the children. It was fenced with a 10 ft cyclone fence and was filled with wood mulch for safety. It had swings, a sand area, and a huge pirate ship that had two- floors for playing. The interior of my building was set up with learning stations; we had computers, game stations, a library area, an art area, sand and water tables, a TV and video area, a play dough and clay area, and a science area. The facility also had a kitchen for breakfast and lunch equipped with school cafeteria tables that would fold up after meals. The bathrooms were in the back of the facility. We had separate restrooms for the boys and girls, each set up with 3 stalls, each with three different-sized toilets. Toddler toilet, junior, and standard size. The boy's room also had a urinal.

There was a separate rest room, handicapped accessible for the staff. My office was also in the rear. We had a large counter upon entrance in the front where customers could sign in and out each day. My space was licensed for 72 children! It was totally professionally designed into the Best Summer Camp and Before and After school program around. In June of 1997, we opened our doors to 45 children to begin our summer camp program. We called our camp program "Kamp Kastle." Between dealing with pain now alternating between both lungs and taking ugly hormones, I beamed with pride! The Kiddie Korral was becoming a Great Success, and my hard work and ambition were finally coming to fruition. Miss Chrissy was officially named my Assistant Director, and we would trade back and forth between the two locations. In the grand scheme of things, life is good, but it would be great if I could get better!

Talent Unlimited

In Kristin's freshman year, she was quite the athlete. She made the varsity soccer team and was in the paper constantly. She scored many goals, and Tim Hawk, who worked for the Gloucester County Times, praised her through all the photos and articles in the newspaper. Not only did she make the Varsity Soccer Team, but she also made the Varsity Basketball Team and Spring Track Team. She had so many rebounds and points in basketball that she was plastered on the front page of the Sports section. Her specialty in Track was the Hurdles, 100-meter dash, and the Long Jump! She was jumping over 16ft. I became her sideline cheerleader for all sports! While she was excelling in sports, Erin was our Pageant Queen and taking vocal lessons with Robert Edwin in Cinnaminson, NJ. She had won the title of Little Miss NJ and competed in a National Pageant in Maryland. She was quite the Little Star!

I was a Proud Mother of both my daughter's successes. Our son Harry was playing baseball and was becoming a good pitcher for his little league team. All was good on the home front for now, with just one small problem: my nagging friend that caused me to spend a week to 12 days a month in pain! Harry and I entertained the idea of adding to our family, but with my illness still looming in the shadows of our lives, we began talking about adoption. I often said I wanted to adopt a baby, but resources in the United States were very limited, especially since I had had 3 children already; our chances were almost null to adopt a baby in the United States.

One day, I was scrolling the internet and found that there was an adoption agency in Cherry Hill, NJ, that was having a seminar to help families adopt children from other countries. Without hesitation, I signed us up. Within 2 weeks, we were sitting in a ballroom at the Hilton Hotel in Vorhees, NJ. We were amongst many other couples that were also interested in adoption. The seminar was very interesting, and we were served lunch and given a packet, which also included an application to adopt a baby. The process looked very tedious, to say the least. The application was

5 pages long, and the fees varied according to which country you chose for adoption. We left with a lot of information and a hell of a lot of decisions to make. We definitely were going to adopt a baby girl, however, what country would we choose? "Reaching Out Through International Adoption" gave us many options. We could adopt a baby girl from China, Russia, Guatemala, or Vietnam. After many long discussions between my husband and I, we chose Russia. Partly because my husband didn't want the child to look so different from us that she would be known as an adopted child throughout life.

However, the main reason we decided to go with a Russian child is because my adopted father's mother, my paternal grandmother, was from Ukraine. So, we delivered the application to the Director, Jeanine, with a $375.00 application fee in July of 1998. We met with her and a wonderful lady named Hannah, who would be our main liaison in our journey to adopt. We began by looking through books of available babies and children. There were hundreds of photos and stories, each one detailing a child's life. It was both heartwarming and surreal to flip through the pages of a book, searching for a child as though we were browsing a Sears catalog to pick out a Christmas gift. The adoption agency had videos we could watch and observe the baby to get a better understanding of what the child's needs would be. Russia had thousands of babies in orphanages throughout areas of Russia. You could not legally adopt a baby from Russia until the baby was 6 months old. This was to ensure that the birth mother did not change her mind. Reaching Out also had pediatricians you could hire that would watch the videos and read the medical reports to tell you what the health needs would be for each child.

Our first choice was a red-headed baby girl who was 6 months old and ready to be adopted. We hired a doctor to look over her medicals, and we were informed she suffered from fetal alcohol syndrome. We decided against her. We continued to go back to Reaching Out once a week to look through the books to find our daughter. It was the end of August when I spotted a little blonde-haired, blue-eyed boy, 8 years old, and dressed head to toe in blue jeans. He was beautiful, I knew right then I was interested, but after having his video translated for us, I was Sold! He was very smart and was practically begging for a Forever Family. He had been on the streets eating from trash cans when the Russian authorities placed him in an orphanage at age 4. His mother is apparently unable to care for him; he became an orphan and has been living in an orphanage for 4 years! I couldn't leave him there, so I talked my husband into adopting him instead of a baby girl.

We now had to be fingerprinted and background checks to be approved. We also had to pay a social worker to do a family study to be approved. The social worker, Leslie, had to inspect our home, the room that our son would sleep in, and go through our financials. We needed 4 references, and our biological children's health records, school reports, and social status. She came out to my school and spoke to my employees, and my husband's boss. The hoops we had to jump through were unbelievable and financially draining. But we were approved and ready to travel to Russia to bring our son home.

Unfortunately, after preparing for our son, we received a phone call from Jeanine telling us our son was already adopted! It was like having a miscarriage, but worse, after all the preparation and having his face and personality etched in my mind, my heart was broken, and I cried for days. My husband convinced me that God had different plans and that it wasn't meant to be, so we returned to the adoption agency and started looking again for a baby girl. It was a day before we would celebrate our 11th wedding anniversary; we found our baby girl; her name was Polina, and she was shy of 5 months old. She was very tiny; she was sitting in a baby seat and looked adorable. We would have to wait until she was 6 months old to travel to bring her home. We had her medicals sent to the pediatrician for review and began the wait once again.

Our pediatrician, Dr. Hoffstetter, specialized in pediatric neurology at Presbyterian University Hospital in New York. She reviewed the medical records for Russian children, translating and explaining their medical histories to us. She assured us that our daughter did not have fetal alcohol syndrome but had experienced cognitive challenges due to being born prematurely, weighing just 2 lbs. at birth. She suffered from microcephaly. She told us she could have learning problems but could not tell us the severity because of how young she was. She told us with proper nutrition and care, she could be fine, but then again, she may suffer from developmental problems. After a couple of days of thought and consideration, we decided she was ours. We decided that God was sending us to save her because, truth be told here, she was only 5.5 lbs. at almost 6 months old. This was a life-saving journey that we were determined to make.

Preparing for Adoption

After redecorating a bedroom for our son Harry and our adopted son, buying two new beds for the bedroom that they would share, and then receiving the bad news that he was already adopted, we now had to redo two bedrooms. We converted the downstairs library into a bedroom for our oldest daughter, Kristin, who was a senior in high school. Erin moved into Kristin's former room, and we set about transforming the small bedroom into a nursery for our baby daughter. This was an ordeal to do over the holidays. Kristin was sponge-painting her walls in a gold and burgundy theme, and she did a fantastic job.

We moved Erin's furniture into the front bedroom and started working on the nursery. We bought a canopy crib, painted the walls a pinky mauve and wallpapered one wall in rose-colored bows. We found a matching crib ensemble and rocking chair adornment to match the wallpaper. Harry built shelves that were painted white over the changing table. We had found a matching curtain for the window, and the room looked like it was made for a Princess. Delicate pink ribbons and bows were prepared for our sweet little princess.

By January, we were all set to bring her home. However, in keeping with the unpredictability of so many events, this moment was no exception. It was a very cold and bitter day in January when Jeanine from Reaching Out called us and told us that our son Victor's adoption fell through because the man who was trying to adopt him had a record of being arrested for abusing a neighborhood child and was turned down to adopt. She wanted to know if we would consider adopting him. I said we were all set to go get Polina now, and she needed us! Jeanine said why not adopt both of them? Well, I'd love to, but I didn't have the money, plus I'm not certain what my husband would want.

She told me she could get us a loan through First Union Bank, and she would cut us a deal if we took both. So when my husband came home from work, with a lump in my throat and my mouth as dry as a desert, I began with Jeanine called today…..to my dismay and surprise, he responded with, "What's one more? Let's Do It!!"

The very next day, we found ourselves at First Union Bank, applying for a $20,000 loan to bring home not one but two children from Russia. To support both of our children, we arranged to send food, formula, and clothing to Russia through Sergei, a contact for Reaching Out in the region who assisted families with the adoption process. We would stay in the home that he and his wife owned when we traveled to adopt. His wife Tanya was at the Ministry of Education in Rostov on Don, Russia, and that is how the Reaching Out Adoption Agency in Russia was born. Both Sergei and Tanya lived in Tom's River, NJ, and their home in Russia would serve many families traveling to adopt babies and children. Part of our requirement to adopt was to send food & clothing to the children we were adopting for 4 weeks prior to our travel.

We also sent pictures to Victor so he could see the family who was adopting him. Everything was taking longer than expected due to the journey becoming two children rather than one. We had to wait for the money from the bank, and they also had to do a regional search for Polina's birth mother because she abandoned her at the hospital 24 hours after birth. After a two-week search, it was determined that she gave a false name to the hospital because she was never found. In Victor's case, his mother had lost all her parental rights due to negligence, and he was free and clear to be adopted.

At the beginning of March, I was delighted by a wonderful surprise—a fabulous baby shower hosted by my dear friend Maryann at her home. She had gathered so many of my friends and relatives to celebrate, and the thoughtfulness of it all was overwhelming. Since we were preparing for two children, the guests brought two gifts, making the occasion even more special. It was a truly beautiful and heartfelt gesture from a cherished friend. She and her husband, John, would both serve as our baby girl's godparents. My sister Kelly and brother-in-law Curt would be Victor's godparents.

By the third week in March of 1999, we received word that everything was ready, our plane tickets were bought, and we were to be at JFK airport in New York by 4 PM on April 3, 1999. Although we were very excited, I was upset that we were leaving on my oldest daughter Kristin's 18th birthday!! Kind of a bittersweet day. Murphy's Law struck again! Not only were we leaving on Kristin's 18th birthday, but the next day was Easter Sunday. I had to prepare and hide Easter baskets in advance so my mother could come over and set them out the next morning.

While the girls weren't too concerned about Easter baskets, Harry Jr., at just 10 years old, still cared a great deal! I was torn over missing these days with my children, but I knew I didn't have any control over the situation. As my parents were driving us to New York to catch our flight from JFK International Airport, I could tell they were feeling a bit worried. After all, we were flying on a huge plane across the ocean to Russia. For my parents who never stepped foot on an airplane, it was an adventure that they would never do! As we got to the gate, carrying a huge suitcase filled with belongings for not only us but for the two children we would be bringing home, I had two small carry-ons and a purse wrapped around my body, which all had to be put down for a BIG Hug and a tearful goodbye. I assured both my parents that we would call them, no matter the time, as soon as we landed.

As I entered the Big International Airliner, tears rolled down my cheeks, and although I was filled with great joy to be finally going to get our children, I also felt sad for my parents' fear and leaving my 3 children at home.

Arriving in Moscow!

After a very long and grueling flight of 10 hours, we finally landed in Moscow. I thought I would have caught some sleep on the plane, but the anticipation of what we were soon to embark on did not allow my mind to be calm enough to sleep. So, as we walked off the plane down the corridor, carrying all our luggage, I was feeling my tired body begin to feel the effects of no sleep. As we walked downhill on a ramp, we were met by the biting cold of a blizzard. Battling the harsh wind and stinging snow, we trudged across a vast, snow-covered field to reach a small commuter plane waiting for us. Moscow's icy weather was relentless, and the snow whipped against our faces as we finally boarded the tiny plane, settling into the first two seats.

The plane held 16 passengers, and as I fastened my seatbelt, I looked at my husband and said, "I'm scared!" He said, as confident as can be, "We'll be fine." It was the scariest 2 hours of my life. I cannot tell you the terror I felt as the plane floated up and down from the turbulence experienced from flying through a blizzard to get from Moscow to Rostov on Don. Throughout the entire flight, I prayed silently while my husband struck up a conversation with a man seated across the narrow aisle. His name was Kenny Shoemaker, a professional National stock car driver who raced from 1948 to 1978. After his retirement, he was honored with an induction into the Hall of Fame by the NYSSCRA. He was professionally known as Shoe and had many stories to tell. Since my husband's family was into building and racing stock cars, he was very interested in race cars and racing. His Uncle Jeep built and raced stock cars from the 1950s to the 1960s until he hired a driver named Bunky Higbee from Fortescue, NJ. He drove Uncle Jeep's car, the red and white #26, and won many championships year after year. So, my husband enjoyed talking with Kenny Shoemaker as I sat with my knees shaking the entire flight!

Finally, we landed again in a field and had to walk down steps off the plane and trudge through the snow to enter a small airport in Rostov On Don.

It was not like our airports in the United States. It was small and only accepted commuter planes that would land in an open field behind the airport building. We entered through the back door and joined a long line at customs to have our entry verified. The process took more than an hour and a half. Afterward, we climbed a small flight of steps to reach street level, where we waited for our driver to arrive and take us to the house where we would be staying. As we waited, my husband, Harry, began talking to a Russian man who spoke some English and told us he was from an area where they were trying to break away from Russia. He was a soldier for Chechnya. He lived in a region called Georgia, and he told us that many people who were from the Chechnya region were fleeing to Taganrog, Russia, to avoid the war that was happening in Chechnya. He told us to be careful while traveling to Taganrog.

It would be hours before we made it through Customs and exchanged United States Currency for Russian Money. However, it would prove to be a blessing at the time. One American Dollar was worth 25 Russian Rubles (dollars). So, needless to say, we were rich in Russia. We waited a couple of hours for our driver to arrive. We were tired and famished! We purchased crackers and a can of soda from a vending machine to curb our appetite. Finally, at dusk, a man named Misha arrived to pick us up; we were literally starving and exhausted. There is a 7-hour time difference between Russia and the United States.

We arrived at the house in which we would call home at 7 PM. We were provided with a cook and housekeeper named Galina. As she prepared our dinner, I called my mother to let her know we had arrived safely. I had to go through an international operator in order to make the call. My mom picked up and accepted the charges, and she said, "OMG, I was really worried! "I told her we were at the house we would be staying and that we had just arrived. She thought we would be calling early in the morning as it was a 10-hour flight. I explained how we had to take a commuter flight to Rostov On Don and all the processes of customs and the money exchange, the wait at the airport for our chauffeur, and this was the first availability of a phone. After a 10-minute call that probably would cost her a fortune, we hung up. While Galina prepared our dinner, we settled in with a glass of wine, unpacked, and got comfortable. I pulled out a journal I had bought before our trip and began documenting everything that had happened since we boarded the jetliner in New York, 15 hours earlier.

Although my tired body craved sleep, I knew my stomach needed   food. Galina prepared a meal for royalty. She made chicken & dumplings with a side of German green beans with bacon. They had wine on the table and a tossed salad. The meal was delicious, and we sat around and chatted with Galina and Misha for an hour during dinner. They both spoke Russian but knew enough English to carry on a conversation. After dinner, we retired to our bedroom for hopefully a good night's sleep. Tomorrow, we will be visiting both our children in two different orphanages in two different regions. Misha would be picking us up at 10 am.

I must have slept like a baby until I was awakened by the smell of coffee and something Galina was cooking in the kitchen. She made us a wonderful omelet filled with cheese and buzhenina (Russian ham) along with fried potatoes and juice, as well as coffee. I do not think I ever ate such a tasty breakfast. She was an exceptional cook and a gracious hostess.

After enjoying the meal and freshening up with a shower, we dressed and were ready promptly at 10 AM when Misha arrived to pick us up. He explained that our journey would begin with a visit to Victor in Novoshakhtinsk, Russia, located northwest of Rostov-on-Don. It felt like it took a very long time to arrive. Most of the trip was desolate through open plains of dusty wheat fields. It was miles and miles of nothing but a two-lane freeway, like something you would see on a Western Movie before civilization took place. After about two and a half hours, we arrived at a cute residential area with modest-sized homes. We drove about a mile until we pulled up to a big stone building that resembled a school from the outside. The orphanage was quite impressive from the outside. But first impressions can fool you. The inside was run down with old furniture that seemed to be from the 1940s. We were led to an office where we met the Director, who only spoke Russian, so Misha acted as the interpreter. The Director asked if we wanted to take Victor today.

Although the adoption court hearing was still two days away, she offered to release him to us immediately if we were open to it. "First, let me introduce you to your son," she said. As we followed her down the hallway, we passed by the bathroom. I was appalled when I looked in the room to see a line of holes in a concrete floor with a pipe above the holes with a handle for flushing. NO toilets, just holes in the floor with water in the holes! Basically, the children had to squat over the holes to go. I felt the tears fill my eyes as we continued to follow the Director to a sitting room to meet Victor. He was dressed in blue jeans and a blue jean jacket, just like the photo we saw in the available children's catalog at the adoption agency. He had beautiful blue eyes and was as handsome as he could be. I hugged him, and he was talking a mile a minute in Russian; I had no idea what he was saying until Misha told us. "What took you so long? I've been waiting a long time for you to come get me."? He had a small bag of clothes over his shoulder, which were the clothes we sent him, and he said in Russian- "Let's Go! I'm ready!" Misha had to tell him to sit down and wait.

We were given paperwork for Victor's medical information since he entered the orphanage four years prior. His birth name was (Vicktor Yankovich Di-Dinken). After all the paperwork was signed, we exited the orphanage and took a photo of Victor with the Director-in front of it, then off to the car we went. Victor shed no tears, and he continued babbling in Russian; he couldn't get in the car fast enough. As soon as we got to the car, Misha said, "Victor, get in, sit down and shut up!!" He then told Victor what he was saying in Russian). We were now going to make a 4-hour trip to Taganrog to meet Nadia. Every 20 minutes or so, Victor would say.... "Sit down and shut up." We would laugh, and he would laugh, too. It was a long trip to Taganrog; it was more congested with traffic, and every 3 miles, there were towers with Militia (police) watching the roads. It felt like I was driving through a military camp, I never saw anything like it.

Misha explained that with all the turmoil in Chechnya and the people escaping to areas in Taganrog, the region was filled with Military Militia. He said they set up checkpoints and that if we were stopped, we were not to speak. We would be Canadians if asked. On top of the Chechnya war, the United States was bombing Yukaslavia, and Russia was sympathetic to the Serbians, so we had to remain silent. Of course, we came to a checkpoint, and Misha got out of the car and explained his destination, and all was good. In less than 20 minutes we pulled up to a bright yellow concrete building that set very close to the Black Sea. Nothing was around, and it looked so deteriorated that it was scary to enter.

As we entered the building, it was a vestibule with a small counter and a few plastic chairs. Misha told the woman we were here to meet our daughter. We were told to sit down, and within 5 minutes, a woman brought her to us. Her birth name was "Mosgova Polina Pavlovna" she was so tiny, she weighed 10 lbs. and she was 10 months old. Her head literally fit in the palm of my hand. She smiled at us and was very happy to be held and kissed. She could hold her head up, but it was obvious that she suffered from malnutrition. My husband shook his head side to side, which she emulated, and shook her head side to side back. Although she looked so fragile, my husband said she was able to show us some signs that she understood by her ability to repeat a jester. We only had 30 minutes to spend with her on our first visit, but we would return again tomorrow before the court. We gave her director 2 quarts of formula as part of our responsibility in the adoption process. Every day we visited, we had to bring 8 diapers and two quarts of formula. We left feeling joy and anticipation to see her the next day before court.

We went back to Rostov On Don, and Misha took us to shop at a flea market, where everyone in the street was trying to give us shots of vodka. We bought Victor a brown leather bomber jacket, and we all bought Russian T-shirts and ate sausage sandwiches from a lunch truck. It was truly a pleasure being treated so

114

wonderfully by the Slavic people. When we came home that night, Galina was preparing another fantastic dinner, and we met Sasha, who was Tanya's brother. He would be our liaison at court and also would be traveling with us back to Moscow to get our children's passports. Tonya was the wife of Serqei and they owned the house we were staying It was a big family affair, and we were blessed to be a part of it. Our dinner was beyond fabulous; she made us steak and mashed potatoes with broccoli and a fresh salad. We retired for the night early because tomorrow was going to be the big day. We would d be leaving early to visit our baby girl so that we could get back in time for our Court hearing. It was scheduled for 2 PM, and all the months of preparation would be finalized tomorrow before dinner.

April 8, 1999-Adoption Day!

We started the day off with another great breakfast made by Galina. She definitely had to be the best cook in Rostov on Don, and she made our trip very heartwarming. She not only prepared our meals but changed our bed sheets daily, washed our dirty clothes, and offered us support daily. She was truly a blessing that made our trip superb in every way possible. After finishing our breakfast, we quickly got ready, and Misha picked us up to visit Polina. It was a two-hour trip, and we had to be back in time for the court at 2 PM. As we made our way to Taganrog, the Military Militia was not as kind this trip.

Apparently, we were stopped because the Militia said Misha drove over the center line on the road! He got out of the car and was talking to the Militia, and as I sat in the back seat with my son Victor, I could feel my legs begin to shake! After a few minutes, Misha got back in the car and told us he was being fined, and without paying the fine, they would not allow us to go. My husband said the fine was $250.00 rubles which in American dollars was $10.00. I got a ten-dollar bill out of my purse and gave it to Misha to pay the fine. He could not have been more appreciative. He said that was his rent for the entire month, and he was overjoyed that we gave him the money. We were on our way once again without losing too much time. We were able to enter the orphanage this visit, and after walking up a large staircase we were brought to a large room with cribs aligning both sides of the room.

There must have been at least 50 cribs in this room all filled with babies that were awaiting adoption. It made my heart sad to see so many babies that were lying in cribs with very little stimulation and some crying for food. The caregiver brought Polina to us, and we went into another room that, by surprise, had carpet on the floor. There were toys in the room, so I took a blanket from the shelf in the room and we laid her on the blanket to play. It was then that I noticed her nose running and her inability to even turn over. She was sick with a cold we were told. When our visit was over, I hugged my baby girl and told her we would be back to get her soon. The Director of the orphanage told us that it would be better to pick her up tomorrow since she was ill, and of course, I wanted to come back after court and pick her up. But Misha told us it was better to pick her up tomorrow prior to leaving Rostov on Don to travel to Moscow to get our children's visas to bring them home.

So, as we left, I felt sad, and the waterworks began. She just looked so frail and weak. Her little face was chapped from her nose running, and she looked at me with sad eyes as if to say…" Please don't leave me here"! The ride back was tough, but we made it to the Court House with time to spare. The Court House was a huge stone building, and as we entered the corridor there were long wooden benches aligning the walls that reminded me of church pews. We walked the hallway until we came to the courtroom, where we were to have our hearing. Sasha was waiting for us outside on a bench. He told us that he would do the speaking and translate everything being said. The Judge would be speaking Russian.

As we entered the room, we sat down and waited for our turn. Many American Couples were waiting to adopt Russian children. The couple that was being heard at the time was from Michigan, and they wanted to adopt a baby girl. As the Judge hit down her gavel, the woman cried! Sasha explained that the man was in the Air Force and was one of the pilots who was bombing Yugoslavia, so the Judge denied the adoption. My knees were shaking now, OMG!!! If the Judge denied us our adoptions, all the money we spent would be lost. There were no refunds! I felt so bad for the couple leaving the courtroom sobbing.

Every couple sitting in this courtroom was waiting to be heard by the judge, awaiting to make their dreams come true. The judge held our future family in her hands. Every couple's adoption journey is unique, but in our case, we already had 3 children and we were asking to adopt two Russian children to add to our family. Would the judge think we were being greedy by wanting to adopt 2 children? Our fate was in her hands. Finally, we heard our names being called, and we moved toward the front of the courtroom.

Sasha approached the Judge offering photos of our family back home, pictures of the bedrooms in which our new children would reside. We sat still in our seats and waited. The Judge was very pleased with our photos, and commented that she felt the children were very lucky to have parents like us. She asked Victor if he wanted to be adopted, and he stood up and said loudly and proudly..."Da!" (The Russian word for Yes). He then... "MaMa & PaPa," as he hugged us. I had a lump in my throat and fought back the tears.

The Judge asked us a few questions, which Sasha translated for us. Basically, we had to say we desired to adopt the children. She asked us if we wanted to change the children's first names. Victor, being 8 years old, we decided to keep his first name, but we opted to change his middle name and last name, of course. Victor would now be Victor Patrick. Next, Polina would be Nadia Lynn. The Judge asked if we wanted to change her birthday since she was so small and developmentally delayed. We decided against that; after all, a birth date is sacred and not to be changed.

Our beautiful daughter was born on June 12th, 1998, by God's Will, and we were not going to change it. The Judge wished us luck and said, "God Bless You and your family." Victor also thanked the Judge and said with a huge smile on his face, "Ya idu domoy !" (I'm going Home!) in English. As we departed the courthouse, Victor was speaking a mile a minute and filled with excitement! Sasha, being the only one who understood what he was saying, translated for us what Victor said. Are we going to the plane now? He was anxious to go home to America, and wanted to leave now! Sasha laughed as he told Victor we would be leaving in the morning after we picked Nadia up from her orphanage. Sasha took us back to the house where we were staying, and Galina joined us in taking Victor to a park. The sun was shining, and the day was filled with joy.

Later that evening, Misha took us to the airport to buy ice cream to celebrate with Victor. The airport was the only place that sold ice cream, as Russian families could not afford the simple luxury of ice cream. We bought 6 aluminum foil slabs of ice cream wrapped up like a Klondike bar in America. It was equivalent to a half gallon of ice cream. Again, Misha could not believe we could spend $10.00 American dollars on ice cream. Victor was astonished at seeing the planes coming and going in the sky and again was chattering away about going on an airplane the next day. We enjoyed our last evening with Galina and Misha, but we would see Sasha in the morning to pick up Nadia and depart from Rostov On Don, and fly to Moscow. April 8, 1999, would go down in our history as the day we adopted our two beloved children.

"All Aboard To Moscow"

We were up bright and early to make one more trip to Taganrog to collect our precious bundle of joy. Galina made us her famous Russian Breakfast before our final jaunt to Taganrog to pick up Nadia Lynn. We were excited and filled with joy to know that in 3 hours, we would be on our way back to Rostov On Don with our sweet daughter and onto the second leg of our journey, which would encompass flying to Moscow to finalize the journey back to America with our two children. On the way to Taganrog, Victor was chatting away with Sasha; of course, we were unaware of what he was saying, but it was a joy listening to him; even though we did not understand what he was saying, we could tell by the smile on his face that is was happy chatter. Finally, the two-hour drive was complete, with no wrinkles in the journey. As we pulled up to the large deteriorating building, we were reminded by Sasha how lucky and fortunate Nadia was that we chose her.

Although we smiled and shook our heads yes, inside, we knew that we were lucky to have her! As the Director handed Nadia to me, all I could do was say Thank you so much, as the tears welled up in my eyes. She was so tiny; she looked like a newborn baby wrapped tightly in a receiving blanket. Her nose was running like a spicket, but she still managed a smile when she looked up at me. The Director wished us luck and told us to have a safe trip home to America. I held her in my arms in the back seat all the way back to Rostov On Don. We gathered all our belongings and said our goodbyes to Galina, thanked her for her hospitality and all the wonderful meals she prepared for us, gave her a big hug, and left her an envelope with a $100.00 tip for all her help. She was overjoyed, and she cried as we left. Sasha took us to the airport in Rostov On Don; again, we had to walk outside to a commuter plane that would fly us to Moscow. As I walked up the steps to enter the plane, I was praying that we would all make it safely to Moscow. The small plane was scary, and I was terrified to have to fly again another two hours on this rickety aircraft, but this time with our two beloved children. Victor was filled with excitement, and he talked a mile a minute to everyone who would listen. Sasha told us he was telling everyone he was going home to America with his Mamma and Papa.

As I sat on the plane, I thanked God for Blessing us with these two beautiful children. As the plane took off, my stomach dropped, and before I knew it, Rostov On Don was out of sight forever! Unlike our flight to Rostov On Don, this plane was filled with many passengers. Sasha explained that many of the passengers were heading to Moscow for work. Rostov On Don was a very small region in Russia that was the main hub for Russian Forces in Ukraine. So, work was limited for the Civilians. Many men would fly 600 miles daily to Moscow to gain employment; some would stay through the work week and fly back to their families on Friday.

However, some would fly back and forth on a daily basis. The thought of two trips daily on this plane would be more than my heart could take. I'd starve to death before I could fly twice a day on this aircraft, which caused my heart to beat rapidly out of my chest! I can tell you when the plane landed safely on the ground in Moscow, I yelled rather loudly, "Amen"! As we exited the plane, the bright sunshine hit us in the face! It was cold but not snowing like the day we left Moscow to fly to Rostov On Don. Sasha quickly led us off the plane and into a large modern airport where he rented a car to drive us to an area where we entered a rinky-dink office on a side street somewhere in Moscow, where we had to prove our identity. Sasha did all the talking, and we just sat and waited, only having to produce our visas to prove we were able to fly home with our children.

After about 20 minutes, we were back in the car and on our way to the Embassy. Upon arriving, we had to park in a lot and walk about 5 blocks to the American Embassy. The Embassy was enormous! Hundreds of people were lined up around its perimeter. The windows were boarded up, and the building was covered in paint-filled graffiti. Russian militia officers stood guard, carrying guns, and Sasha explained that local citizens had vandalized the building, even blowing out all the windows. Because America was bombing Yugoslavia, the Russians were sympathetic to the Serbians and were retaliating by defacing the American Embassy. The destruction was awful, and a pang of fear took my breath away!

As I carried Nadia in a baby sling on my chest, I held Victor's hand very tightly. Sasha was asking questions on where we had to go and what line we had to be in. There were people everywhere. After Sasha found out where we were to go, he told us to follow him. The crowds were enormous, and as we pushed our way through the rat race, I heard my husband yelling my name; when I turned around, the Russian Militia had stopped my husband and wouldn't allow him through. Since Sasha had our Visas, my husband was being held hostage! I had to run up to Sasha to go back and get him. Because of the conflict from America bombing Yugoslavia, we were in harm's way! It literally was a scary situation that I will never forget! After more than an hour of bone-chilling fear, we finally made our way into the American Embassy, where we received our children's visas. As we got back in the car, I took out a bottle to feed Nadia. And as she gobbled down her bottle, I let out a sigh of relief. Leave it again to Murphy's Law to have us in Russia to adopt our children while Our country was bombing Yugoslavia!

Sasha took us to Red Square. Red Square is the equivalent of Washington, DC, in the United States. We were able to view all the statues of Russian Leaders through time. Venders were there and we were able to get a bite to eat. After leaving Red Square, we were driven to the place where we would spend two days but three nights, awaiting our flight home. We were going to be staying with an older couple in an apartment. The woman was a school teacher, and her husband was an electrical engineer. Tom and Helen who were bilinguals, and both spoke Russian and English, which would be a real blessing for our family. Upon pulling up to this high-rise apartment in the city section of Moscow, the area was observed as not being the safest part of the city. Upon coming to the entrance to the building, we noticed bars on the door and bars on the windows. The foyer was unkept and kind of dirty. On the back wall was an elevator. However, unlike the elevators in the United States, this elevator looked like a cage. It was very small, and literally black iron bars surrounded a small floor that a key was needed to open the cage to enter. A key was also needed to make the elevator move up and down. Sasha had to call the apartment so Helen could come down to bring us up. She was a nice lady that, I believe, was in her early sixties. She was very friendly and greeted us in a welcoming manner. As we entered the elevator, I felt a pang of insecurity, wondering how this elevator was going to hold all 6 of us. Before I gave it another thought, Helen said I'm going to take your wife and children up, and I'll be right back to get you two men.

As the elevator rose, I could see the outside through the windows in the back of the elevator. It was really a very nice view. Helen stopped at the 5th floor and put the key in the lock to open the elevator so we could exit to a hallway with a steel door that entered her apartment. She told me to have a seat in her living room until she went back down to get the men. The apartment was beautiful and very big. It was decorated with a Victorian flare. The Dining room furniture was amazing, with a big beautiful Victorian Chandelier that hung over the beautiful mahogany table. I undressed Nadia from her snowsuit and helped Victor take off his coat and hat when I heard the front door open and my husband chatting with Helen. The apartment was warm and inviting, and Helen invited us into her kitchen, where she prepared hot cocoa and snacks for us to enjoy. Her kitchen was compact but lovely. We sat down in a built-in nook with a few windows to look down through to the city. She told us that she and her husband had lived here for 25 years. While she taught at a local school her husband worked for a big electric company as an engineer. They started opening their home to couples adopting children from various regions in Russia. They had no children of their own but found it heartwarming to assist in helping couples adopt children.

She informed us that Victor spoke perfect Russian and that he was very smart. It was a delight to have her translate for us. We were able to ask Victor questions, and he was able to tell us what was on his mind. He was very excited but anxious to get to

America. We learned so much with Helen able to translate back and forth. I just wondered how it would work when we returned home with no translator and a big communication gap between us. We already prepared the school system that Victor would be coming home and would need tutoring to learn English. We enrolled Victor in school, and he was ready to go. He was in the 3rd grade, and Helen mentioned that he was advanced and very intelligent for his age. We were happy to hear this, as children living in orphanages in Russia usually are delayed and many times have learning disabilities due to malnutrition and circumstances from a lack of love and support. Hopefully, Victor will thrive when he gets home. Nadia was very delayed; she was 10 months old and appeared as a newborn baby, barely able to hold her head up. She was only currently drinking formula from a bottle, which I believe was very limited in her orphanage. We were dressing her in premature baby clothes, and her head was so small it fit in the palm of my hand.

However, she was a good baby; she slept well, drank her bottle, and burped easily, and she was very pleasant. Always ready to greet me with a smile. We knew she was very delayed in development, and she had a nasty cold that needed our pediatrician to treat as soon as we got home. Our flight was set to depart on Thursday, April 15th, at 10:30 AM, and I had already arranged a visit with the pediatrician for Friday afternoon to check on the children. I was relieved knowing I'd be able to get any medication needed to treat Nadia. The evening arrived quickly after dinner, and the bedroom we slept in was just off the kitchen. It had a a queen bed for us and a twin bed for Victor. Helen also had a bassinet set between the beds for Nadia. We retired early as it was a very busy day filled with stress and anxiety. The rest of our time in Moscow was spent in the apartment playing games and talking. We never left the apartment since we arrived until it was time to go to the airport.

The shuttle van was scheduled to pick our family up at 9:30 AM Thursday morning. Our alarm was set for 7:45 AM to give us time to get ready to leave. Nadia has slept through the night every night since we got her. We awoke bright-eyed and bushy-tailed, happy to be going home! We were drinking coffee in the kitchen when Helen's phone rang; it was our transport calling to tell us there was a change of plans and he would be here in 30 minutes to pick us up. We buzzed around the apartment, throwing last-minute things into our huge suitcase. There was no time to waste—we had to be ready to go as soon as the transport called. We had accumulated quite a bit more than expected, with all the shopping for the children and gifts for family and friends. My husband struggled to close the zipper on the overstuffed suitcase. But that was only the beginning of our nightmare. When transport called to inform us, they were downstairs waiting for us, my husband picked up the suitcase that did not have rolling wheels on it and pulled his back out! He was in agony and could barely move.

Somehow, we had to get this suitcase down to the van with two children and my husband, who could barely stand up! Helen had to call the maintenance man for the apartment to come and get the suitcase and then help my husband down to the van. He moaned the entire ride to the airport. When we arrived at the airport, the transport got my husband a wheelchair to get him into the airport. This was a real live nightmare; I had Nadia on my chest in a baby sling and my purse and carry-on over my neck and holding Victor's hand. My husband was being wheeled to Customs, and me trailing behind. "Hail Mary full of Grace, help me get through this rat race!"

After clearing Customs, they wheeled my husband onto the plane and settled him in, where he would remain for the entire flight home. That left me on my own to care for both children during the 10-hour journey. Little did I know how challenging those next 10 hours would be! Nadia had a severe infection that seemed to be affecting her ears, making things even more difficult. She screamed for hours, and Victor, who spoke Russian, kept trying to tell me he had to go to the bathroom, which, of course, I did not understand, so he, of course, soaked his pants and the seat he had to sit in for hours! I kept trying to feed Nadia her bottle to pacify her. The flight attendant said sucking would relieve her ear pressure. It did help until her belly was full, and she didn't want to drink anymore. She screamed and cried so loudly that I think the passengers on the plane hated me. I kept trying to shove the pacifier in her mouth until she finally cried herself to sleep. Murphy's Law got me good this time.

Home of the Brave

We finally landed in JFK Airport a little after 1:30 PM and I recall never feeling so relieved in my life. We made it back safely, but not in one piece. Our "head of the household" was broken and in dire pain. They carried my husband off the plane in a carrier chair, requiring the strength of two men to manage. My parents were waiting at the gate to welcome us home. My dad turned to my mom and said, "Joanie, I just saw Harry being carried into a room over there." My Mom's reply was, "You're crazy! Harry is with Dana," But Dad was right. I had to go through Customs with the children by myself. It was a grueling process with Nadia again in the baby sling on my chest and Victor talking a mile a minute in Russian, in which I didn't understand one word he was saying! Not to mention, carrying a purse and carry on hanging over my back, so it didn't hit Nadia in the sling on my chest. It was a stressful 40 minutes that seemed like hours before I was able to greet my parents at the gate. My Dad went out to get the car and pulled it up to a door where they brought my husband out in a wheelchair. My Mom sat in the back seat with Victor and me to allow my husband to sit in the front seat. There was absolutely no way he could have maneuvered his way into the back seat. We had a 3-hour drive from JFK Airport in New York to get home. My mother held Nadia to allow me to catch a few Zzzz's of sleep.

Finally, at 5:45 PM, we pulled into our driveway- "Home Sweet Home"! Our oldest daughter, Kristin, prepared a homecoming dinner and invited my Aunt Sis and our Dear Friends, Mary Ann and John, who were all there to welcome us home and meet our darling children. It took every ounce of strength to get Harry in the house. He got in the family room and laid on the floor to relieve the pressure on his back. He ate his dinner lying on the floor. Meanwhile, Nadia was being passed around for everyone to hold and cuddle. I took Victor upstairs to show him the bedroom he would share with his brother, Harry Jr. The room was decorated with a Phillies and Flyers theme, featuring two twin beds with matching comforters that complemented the border along the ceiling. Victor was thrilled, but what he was saying, only God knew. The celebration ended at about 9 PM when my husband announced he had to go to bed; the pain was excruciating, and it had been a long day. We had a busy day coming tomorrow, but I never imagined just how crazy the next day was going to be.

At 6:00 AM, I was awakened by my husband, who informed me that he needed me to drive him to the hospital. I said we have to get our older children off to school and get Victor and Nadia dressed and fed first. I had no clue how this was all going to work; I had to get Victor and Nadia to the pediatrician by 1:30 PM. Somehow, I got everything done, and after they admitted Harry to the hospital, I took the children to the pediatrician. Nadia weighed in at 10lbs. 3 ozs., she was in the 10th percentile for weight and the 25th percentile for height. I was told she had a punctured eardrum from an infection that was untreated for too long. All the fluid in her ear and the flight home probably caused the punctured eardrum. I also learned that she had rickets. I had learned about rickets in college but thought it was eradicated in the United States.

However, Nadia was born in Russia, a poor country without the same resources as the United States. Rickets is a disease caused by a lack of vitamin D. This disease causes a softening and weakening of the bones in children. It also causes delayed growth, delayed motor skills, pain in the spine, pelvis, and legs, and muscle weakness. Nadia exhibited all signs. The doctor gave me a script for antibiotics, vitamins, a cough syrup and told me he was having a nebulizer delivered to our home, which I would be giving her 3 treatments a day. He told me to feed her formula only. He wanted her to get as much vitamin D as possible. Baby cereal would fill her belly, and she would be less likely to drink the formula.

As I tried to process all this information, the doctor began examining Victor. As I yet had a chance to catch my breath over Nadia's prognosis, I was stunned when the Doctor told me that Victor had a roach deep in his ear canal that needed surgery to remove! The doctor did not see movement of this roach, and he

128

felt it was probably dead, but he couldn't be positive, and either way, it needed to be removed as soon as possible. He called his ears, nose, and throat pediatric surgeon, and surgery was scheduled for Monday Morning, April 19th.

As I drove home in despair, I called my assistant, Chrissy, to see how everything was going at my school. She assured me that everything was going well, and I thought to myself, Thank God something is going right. After getting home and managing to feed and settle five children, I called my mother to ask if she could come over to watch them so I could head to the hospital and check on my husband. While Kristin or Erin probably could have handled it, given Nadia's illness and Victor's communication challenges, I felt it required the expertise of the ultimate Domestic Queen—my mother.

As I drove to the hospital, I blared the radio and tried to alleviate all the stress and anxiety I was feeling. As Cher was singing…" Believe" I was believing her words. Didn't know if I was strong enough, but prayed I was going to be. I pulled into the parking lot of the hospital, locked my doors and walked toward the hospital front door. I don't know what I was expecting to learn when I saw my husband, but I know that I was hoping he would be coming home. When I entered his room, he was watching TV and was lying on his side to avoid the pain in his lower back. I waited for him to talk to me about his condition prior to telling him the grim news about our children. He began by asking me how the kids were. I avoided his questions and asked him how he was doing. Of course, his answer was lousy. He said they did an MRI and found 3 ruptured discs that needed surgery to fix. He was given pain meds for the pain and was scheduled for surgery Monday Morning.

I responded with "You are kidding "! Then I told him about Victor's surgery and that I couldn't be in two places at once. I felt very annoyed and angered that the two of them would be having surgery at the same time. What are the chances of this? Murphy's Law has got me again! To make matters worse, my chest was hurting, and my period was coming. I drove home from the hospital feeling defeated. My mother agreed to come over and watch Nadia Monday morning when I took Victor to the hospital for his surgery. Maybe with any luck, tomorrow would be a better day.

"Under the Knife"

In spite of the commotion going on around me, the weekend flew by with a few trips to the hospital to visit my husband. Most of the weekend was spent unpacking and getting the house organized in preparation for the busy week ahead. My mother arrived at 7:15 AM on Monday to care for Nadia while I took Victor to the hospital for his surgery. The older girls had already left for school, and Harry Jr. would be leaving in 35 minutes, giving my mother some time to spend with Nadia. Before leaving, I made a quick call to my husband and wished him good luck with his surgery and told him I'd see him soon. The hospital was only 15 minutes away, and the entire ride, Victor was chatting away in the back seat of my Toyota 4-Runner. If only I knew what he was saying! I said a quick prayer silently as I drove, asking God to watch over both Victor and my husband; I also asked for help to get through this day without insult.

Victor's surgery was being done as an outpatient, so with the Grace of God, this should be quick and easy. There was no wait, and Victor was taken to surgery as soon as I checked him in. I sat down with my book in hand, but I think I only managed to read one chapter before the doctor came out to talk to me. Victor was in recovery, and they only sedated him slightly, twilight sedation, he called it. He told me the roach was dead and that it was successfully removed with no harm to his eardrum. He gave me a script for ear drops that I was to give him twice a day to avoid infection. That was it: no complications, no long-term effects on his hearing.

Great News! After calling my mom to give her the good news, I asked her if she would mind if I dropped Victor off to her so I could run to the hospital and see my husband. She agreed but with a bit of hesitation because of the language barrier. When we arrived home, I saw my father's truck parked on the curb; my mother called him to come help her with the troops, which I guess was a good thing. I called my assistant Chrissy to check on everything at the school and then off to the second hospital to visit my husband. By the time I arrived, his surgery was over, and he was actually sitting up in the bed eating lunch. What a relief to see him eating and sitting up, and he could move his toes! My prayers were answered and it seemed like a heavy weight was lifted off my shoulders.

Shortly after he finished lunch, we were both surprised by two visitors who came to visit. Our social worker, Leslie and Hannah, who was the biggest support to us during our adoption journey. Both had heard about Harry's injury and decided to come visit. They were both astonished when I told them about Victor's early morning surgery to remove a dead roach, and everything we endured since arriving home. The visit ended when Harry's doctor came in to speak to him. The doctor explained the procedure that was performed, which was called Kyra pi pan. It was an old-school procedure where this ancient medication was inserted into his spine with guided imaging technology. He had a tiny incision in his back to allow the camera to see the area of the spine that was injured, and with a large syringe, they injected the Kyra Pi pan medication into his spine.

The medication was designed to dissolve the damaged disc and fill the area with a synthetic material to replace its function. The doctor explained that the treatment was unpredictable— sometimes it worked, and sometimes it didn't. We were facing a 50/50 shot. The good news was that he was releasing Harry the next day as long as no complications occurred before then. As I drove home from the hospital, I was relieved that this day was almost over and hopeful that my husband would be among the 50 percentile that the surgery would be successful. My parents were glad to see me arrive home and said they saved me a couple of slices of pizza that they ordered for dinner.

As I put my head on the pillow at the end of the day, I quietly thanked God, and before I knew it, the alarm was ringing, and another day had dawned. After getting the children off to school, I put the cartoons on for Victor to watch as I fed Nadia. After Nadia finished her bottle, I put her in her swing and called Harry at the hospital. The news couldn't have been better. The doctor had already been in to see him, and he was given the green light to come home! I got myself and the children ready and went off to the hospital to pick up my husband. Thankfully, they brought him to the door in a wheelchair so that I didn't have to bring our two children into the hospital. Now we would go home and all be together to live happily ever after. That is for now.

Party like it's 1999!

Hard to believe, but our oldest daughter Kristin was graduating from High School! We threw her a Big Graduation Party and entertained over 100 people. We rented a big outdoor tent and had tons of food. It was a proud day for me and a happy day for Kristin. She was filled with joy and anticipation of going away to college in the fall. She had received two scholarships to play soccer in college, which she turned down. She was done with sports and wanted to go to West Chester University in Pennsylvania in the fall.

So, this would be the last summer we would have her home with us. This party would be a really big celebration of her vast achievements. As I hurried around serving our guests, one of my friends told me our son Victor was drinking beer from the keg!!!! When I scolded Victor, he replied…" Sorry Mamma, in Russia it's ok, in America it's Bad!!!!! Thank God, we caught him before he consumed enough to be drunk! Our family was filled with surprises.

The Long and Winding Road

As the days passed, hubby slowly but surely recovered. I called the elementary school to get Victor started going to school. He had finished his medication, and I needed him to go to school. I had neighbors knocking on my door, complaining he was going into their yard and jumping on their trampoline, and with the communication gap, I was strained, so I called Sergei for help. He talked to Victor on the phone to explain to him that he was not permitted to enter the neighbor's yard and jump on their trampoline. It was time for me to go back to work soon, and I needed Victor in school. The school had known for months that Victor was coming home and would be attending school.

Apparently, someone dropped the ball, and they were not prepared for Victor. After testing him, they decided it would be in his best interest to put him back in second grade rather than third grade, where he was in Russia. So, he entered the 2nd grade, and the horror began. Victor spoke very little English, and the school had made no arrangements to hire an interpreter or support person of any kind. It was a very difficult situation for him, especially the day he had to use the restroom. His teacher did not understand him, so he ran out of the room to the bathroom to avoid having an embarrassing accident. The school called me at my preschool, requesting I come to pick him up. After a few days home and calling the school demanding they educate my son, he returned to school only to be placed in a computer lab with a teacher's aide, where he played games on the computer all day!

This was not acceptable for my son, so my husband and I ended up having to hire and pay a Russian teacher who lived in Mullica Hill who would tutor Victor at my preschool for 6 months. By the end of the summer, Victor was speaking fluent English and was ready to enter the third grade. He was a smart and cheerful little boy. Not to mention handsome with his blonde hair and big blue eyes! He brought so much pride to my heart, watching him achieve so much in so little time. He was a joy to our family and a Great Blessing from God. Things were going well for the most part.

I had to call Early Intervention for Nadia because of her delay in development, and I had a therapist come out to my preschool to work with her 2 mornings a week. John was a delight and helped build back Nadia's weakened muscles in her legs due to the rickets she had. When she tried to walk, her left arm would shake, so it took some time for her to achieve the ability to walk. I think she was walking by 15 months, which was a great achievement for a baby who could barely hold her head up at 10 months of age. It was a trying time for a while, but our family was finally coming together. Everyone was settled in, and before we knew it, we were packing Kristin's room for her August departure to West Chester University. She was full of excitement, but I shed a few tears as we left her at the University. My five children's household would now become four. Little did I know that after one semester at West Chester, Kristin would return home and transfer to Rowan University. She did not like living in a dorm room with two other girls. The room was so crowded, and she was not happy there. So, we went back to pick her up before the Christmas break, and I once again had all my children under one roof.

The End of the 1900s

It was going to begin a new century, and we would celebrate the end of the old in St Louis, Missouri, with my biological family. This would be a New Year's Eve filled with anticipation and fear. The rumors were surfacing that when the clock struck midnight to begin the year 2000, the world would go crazy. The predictions were that the computer systems would crash and the electrical power would cease and the banks would shut down, and we would become a crippled world. So, as we packed our bags to get ready for our trip to St Louis, we were a bit concerned, not only about the rumors but because our older girls were not coming, so they would be home alone.

Also, we were flying, so if the world's electrical and computer systems shut down, we could be stranded in Missouri. However, we wanted to introduce our two new children to everyone, and it's been almost a decade since we visited, so as we landed in St Louis, we were convinced everything would be fine.

At 11:00 pm I called my Mom in NJ and wished her a Happy New Year. Eastern Standard Time was an hour ahead of Central Time, so when she answered the phone and told me nothing crazy happened at midnight, I was certain all the predictions were bogus, and life would continue as usual. As we raised our drinks and offered cheers for the New Year- we were now celebrating the year 2000!!!! We were blessed.

Happily Ever After

As I think about the meaning behind "happily ever after," I have to pinch myself to realize it's not a dream. Everything was going well in 2000. I was running two childcare facilities and making more money than ever. My husband was working as a Superintendent for a contractor in Swedesboro, NJ. He was doing financially well also. Our children were all doing fantastic and life was as good as it gets. I still suffered every month from severe chest pain from thoracic pulmonary endometriosis, but my family was doing well in spite of this horrible disease I was suffering. I kept hoping that one day soon, I would find a doctor who could cure me. In the meantime, I thanked God for all our blessings and continued to run my successful childcare business. It was a challenge for me with two facilities, but they were only 4 miles apart. I had my preschool that housed infants up to age 3, and then a facility we called "Kiddie Korral for the Big Kids," which would occupy our pre-K age 4 to before & afterschool children to age 13.

I had two rents to pay, two head teachers, one in each building. An Assistant Director to help me run two buildings, not to mention, two electric bills, two gas bills, two phone bills, and basically double the expenses for two facilities rather than one. My problem was finding a location large enough to fulfill the enrollment. In the childcare business, the money is in the numbers, and the numbers are in the space. The State of NJ Licensing required 35 square feet of space per child enrolled. So, finding a location large enough was my goal. Basically, some financial obligations, such as rent, electricity, gas, telephone, advertising, etc., were not based on our enrollment but, more importantly, did not matter whether we had 25 children or 100.

However, the State mandated how many staff members were needed depending on enrollment. For example, babies from 6 weeks to 18 months required one staff member for 4 children. Needless to say, with an Infant room with 12 babies, I had 3 staff. The Toddlers 18 months to age 3 required 1 staff member for 6 children; our 3-year-olds required 1 staff member for 10. Our 4-

year-old Pre-K needed 1 staff for 12 children. The before & after-school children were 1 staff member to 18 children. So, between my two facilities, I had 17 staff on payroll, not including myself. I had grown exponentially in 12 years. But I was also growing weary and tired. I knew it was also becoming a financial burden, having double the expenses. I was determined to find a way to have enough space at one location to license 100 children. I remember learning in college that the magic number in childcare was 100. I believe it was mathematically decided that with 100 children, you would be making the highest profit after all expenses were paid. So rather than two facilities, one licensed for 39 children, and the other for 72, I needed one facility large enough for 100 children. (100 x's 35 sq ft) that's a building 3500 sq ft.!

Not to mention bathrooms, offices, and space for heating and utilities would not count in that space, so I am looking for a building at least 3800 sq ft. The NJ State Licensing even had rules for toilets & sinks that were needed per headcount; even 15 infants would constitute 1 toilet, which you know an infant will never use a toilet! It was a tough business to operate and meet all the licensing rules and regulations, but it is even tougher business to make a profit! So, we decided to renovate the Strip Mall location in Sewell to accept infants up to age 13 and close the Mantua location. Although it felt like I failed, I knew it was financially the right decision. It would prove to be the right decision until it wasn't.

April's Miracle

We finally had all the daycare children in one location. The renovations were quite extensive; we had added two large bathrooms, one for the boys, which offered 3 toilet stalls with 3 sized toilets (primary, elementary, and standard). It also offered 1 small urinal. The other was for the girls, which offered 3 stalls with the 3 different-sized toilets also. They both had 3 sinks, which I learned are called 3 water closets; we also had a water fountain installed for the children. We had to build walls to make an infant room and a toddler room. We had large windows installed in the rooms so that parents could look in and watch their babies play before leaving for work. We had a professional counter built at the vestibule, and my office was behind the counter. We had a small cafeteria area with cafeteria tables equipped with benches that folded up, and served as dual uses, our preschooler's lunch room, as well as the before & afterschool classroom. The expenses were much easier managed and the State licensed the facility for 78 children. So, we were licensed for 6 more children than the building was originally licensed for.

However, I gave up my office to do so. Small price to pay when the finances improved considerably. I was less burdened, so this lent me more freedom and less stress. That is until April 27, 2000, at approximately 4:30 PM, when the telephone rang and my daughter Kristin answered. I heard her say oh no, and I could tell something was wrong. She hung up the phone and said Dad was in a bad accident; at first, I thought she meant my Dad, and she said...." no, your husband"! Well, I think my heart stopped when she said we had to leave immediately to get to Cooper Trauma Center, where my husband, "my Prince Charming," was being airlifted. She went back to tell the staff, and then she drove me to the hospital because I was a wreck and in no shape to get behind the wheel. I cried and prayed all the way to the hospital, making promises to God of all the changes I'd make if he allowed my husband to be okay. I think we made it in less than 25 minutes!

As I sat in the waiting room for a doctor to come out and talk to me, my heart was beating rapidly for at least 10 minutes, and as I tried my best to keep it together, truth be told, I was shaking terribly! My mother and Aunt Sissy arrived just as the doctor came out and called me to the back. With a loud, tearful cry, I asked, "Is my husband okay?" He said I'm taking you back to see him, and I stopped walking and said, Dr is he alive? He looked at me and said yes he's alive, let's go back. I guess I had watched too many movies where the person had died, and they were bringing the spouse back to say Goodbye. I was scared out of my Witt's.

However, when we entered the room in the Trauma Center, he was alive and awake. I just started balling when I saw him; it was a stress release and a "Thank You, God" moment, if ever there was one in my life. He had glass in his arms and hands that a nurse was trying to remove. They had machines hooked up to him, monitoring his heart and blood pressure. He had a hospital gown on because the paramedics cut his clothes off at the accident scene. His face still had blood on it from a cut on his forehead, but he was awake and talking. They had already performed a CAT scan of his brain, which was normal. They were sending him for X-rays to look for broken bones. But the doctor said he was a very lucky man. Harry said nobody would help me at the scene. He kept asking for help from the crowd that gathered at the scene, and he heard one man say- "Don't touch him; he's too Bad."! He said he was crying out, "Help Me"! then Uncle Jimmy was there, and he told me I needed to get out of the truck cause gas was leaking from it; you need to get out, Harry! My husband said that's when I busted the back window in my truck to get out!

The truck had flipped 3 times and was on its roof. Apparently, an 18-year-old man ran the stop sign and hit my husband's driver-side door, traveling 50 miles an hour or more. My husband was not wearing a seat belt, and the impact threw him on the passenger's side floor! Had he been wearing a seat belt, he would not have survived! My husband was lying on the roof of the truck, trying to break his back sliding window with his feet! Finally, he reached down on the seat, grabbed his hammer, busted the window, and rolled on the ground. The truck had landed on an embankment, and he was lying on the grass when the paramedics arrived. They called for the helicopter, and he said he heard them saying I hope this guy makes it! The roof of his truck was almost on the seat of the cab. He had hammers and saws, and all kinds of power tools in the cab, all of which could have killed him had they hit him in the head! They told him in the helicopter that if not for his roof racks, he would have died right there. He was a lucky man and I felt like the luckiest wife alive. He would have to remain in the hospital for tests, but so far so good. The doctor was concerned about organ damage or needing surgery. So, I was not leaving him until I knew he was going to be okay. I went out to ask Kristin if she could pick up the kids from school and take them home. Kristin informed me that my friend Mary Ann had already picked them up, was feeding them dinner, and planned to drop them off later. Thank God for my wonderful friend Mary Ann and my daughter being there for me.

My next problem was figuring out how I'd get home from the hospital. My mother offered to take Kristin back to the school to get her car, but Kristin wanted to go back and see Harry. While my mother and Kristin visited Harry, I sat with Aunt Sissy. It was then that she told me my Uncle Jimmy, who had been battling cancer and had lost an eye and half his nose to the disease, had passed away at 4:16 this afternoon. Oh my God, I cried. Did you know Harry just told me Uncle Jimmy was at the accident and told him he needed to get out of the truck now! I just thought he was probably knocked out or imagining Uncle Jimmy. Aunt Sissy looked at me with tear-filled eyes and said I guess he had one more job to do before he went to heaven. Do you think I could go back to see Harry after your Mom and Kristin come out? I leaned over and hugged her, and said, "Of course you can." God spared my husband but took my Uncle. My Aunt and Father lost their brother, but Jesus sent my Uncle Jimmy, who saved my husband. Anyone who saw my husband's truck after this awful accident would agree that a miracle was received that day.

Mayhem Madness

I vowed to God that I would attend Mass every Sunday, and I kept that promise. No matter how busy life became or what challenges arose, I made it a priority to attend Mass every Sunday morning. Once my husband was released from the hospital and felt well enough, he began joining me, attending in his wheelchair. We would take our younger children with us and sit in the quiet room with other parents with young children. My husband was raised Methodist, and I was raised Catholic, but for him, it was all about being thankful to God for sparing his life. So, it was now a ritual every Sunday morning; we would attend mass at Incarnation Church. I could feel my spirituality becoming stronger, and I felt closer to God. Things were still a challenge for our family because my husband could not go back to work, and we began falling behind on our bills.

Between my lung problems and his back problems, we were beginning to feel a great deal of pressure trying to cope with our expenses. Prayer is what kept me going. However, as time went on we were growing bigger in debt. We had credit cards run up to the max, trying to stay afloat. My husband hired a lawyer to file suit against the driver who hit him, but that could be years before it settled. I would go to work in the morning and come home two or three times a day to help my husband get to the bathroom and give him his medication and lunch before running back to work.

It was a very trying time for our entire family. It would be over a year before he was walking again, and going from two incomes to one has proven to be disastrous. To make matters worse, the lawyer informed us that the 18-year-old driver who hit my husband carried the state minimum amount of auto insurance, $15000. So, we were going to drown in debt! Somehow, we made it through the year, but by the beginning of 2001, we were living hand to mouth. I seemed to be robbing Peter to pay Paul and it was a merry-go-round I desperately needed to get off! Then we were hit with another bombshell in August of 2001; my mother-in-law, who had been suffering from Alzheimer's, passed away at only 68 years. My husband was devastated, and it just seemed like our life was falling apart. We needed to figure this out, we needed to make some major changes in order to sustain our family's stability, as well as our marriage that seemed to be crumbling like everything else around us.

The madness continued when I received a letter from the landlord of the shopping center where my school was that rent was increasing by $2000 per month. This was going to put us behind financially big time. It just seemed like Murphy's Law had its grip on us so tight we couldn't move! All I could do was pray. In October of 2001, a "for sale" sign went up in front of a beautiful Victorian property on Main St in Barnsboro, NJ. I had admired that building for many years, but what made this property even better was that it was a daycare center that closed. But, our credit was getting pretty bad, bills were late, and I being the only bread-winner at the time, my husband was still not back to work. How could we possibly buy it? It turned out that the man who owned it was my husband's old boss, so we made a deal to rent it, with an option to buy it within 5 years. The property needed work in order to move to this location; it was dirty, and the whole interior needed to be painted. Not to mention that I needed to make classrooms to be licensed for all the children I had enrolled. The old tenant was strictly family care, and I was a licensed preschool.

I separated the children by age, therefore calling for separated classrooms. My husband got his brothers to come help, and it took us 3 months to get all the work done and have NJ State Licensing come out to inspect and license me. The problem was this building was smaller than the preschool in the shopping center, I couldn't close the Timberline Location until I could find a way to gain more space. So here I am again, running two locations. This was not the game plan, and I couldn't call this building Kiddie Korral without adding to the name. Instead, I called the Main St Location "Kiddie Korral Kastle" because it looked like a castle. I continued to operate the Timberline Location, as I had till August before the rent would increase.

We decided to buy a modular classroom, which would allow 17 more children, but we needed to get approval from the township to do so. I also needed to convert the office space on the second floor into space for a pre-k classroom. But where would my office be? We ordered a shed and had it renovated into an office complete with heat and air conditioning. It was placed at the end of the walkway with beautiful glass sliding doors. In the meantime, we were enrolling new children at the Main St Kastle, and my husband met with the President of the Planning Board for the Township to gain approvals for the modular classroom. His grandchildren were enrolled in our school and were happy to help us. It was a done deal! Labor Day weekend, we got as many friends and family as we could gather and moved out of Timberline Shopping Center. This will mark the fourth location for Kiddie Korral. Now known as Kiddie Korral Kastle.

Hubby joins the Kastle.

In 2003, I was having a lot of health issues; my endometriosis was now in my left lung, and the saga was back. I went to a Dr at Jefferson in Philadelphia, who would place me on medication that would shut down my adrenal gland. The plan was that without a working adrenal gland, it would shut down my hormones, which would stop the endometriosis from growing, and possibly, it would die off and keep my lung from collapsing. However, this medication was toxic to my mental health. I was basically being put in instant menopause, hot, cold, happy, sad, depressed, and crying over anything and everything! The mood swings were gigantic, and my ability to function was deteriorating. Running a business and having a family was proving to be too difficult.

Again, the doctors tried an estrogen patch to help me with the night sweats and mood swings. However, even the lowest dosage of estrogen collapsed my lung in a matter of hours! So, my husband took on more responsibilities at the school; he started by getting his CDL License to become our driver for school-aged children. We were using the modular classroom for before and after-school elementary children, and although we had busing through Mantua Township, we had children from Pitman, Glassboro, Deptford, and Washington Township Schools that needed transportation to school and picked up after school. So, Mr. Harry was our official bus driver and was on the payroll at Kiddie Korral Kastle. We were making this work, and at the mere age of 43, I was officially in menopause!

Barely Floating

By 2005, we had accumulated $70,000.00 on credit cards, trying to save our home. Although Kiddie Korral Kastle was doing well, losing my husband's income was purely devastating to our budget. Although he was making a paycheck from Kiddie Korral, we were still falling behind, and in 2005, we filed personal bankruptcy to get rid of credit card debt and medical bills that were mounting through the roof! Between my illness and his injuries caused by the accident, we had accumulated over $60,000.00 in medical bills. The only way out was to file bankruptcy and reorganize. We remortgaged our house after the bankruptcy was through, and we were off to a new start. The Kiddie Korral Kastle was doing very well, and we were filled to capacity with a large waiting list. Everything was coming up roses for us. When summer approached, we decided to have a summer camp for kindergarten through age 13. "Kamp Kastle"

was born after the Pre-K class graduated. Every year our enrollment would drop in the summer, when the preschool would end. Summers were tough. So, I made a summer camp curriculum filled with trips for the children 4 days per week. We hired magicians and different entertainment on Fridays because that was the only day we stayed on location. Mondays were Park Day, and the children would bring a bag lunch from home, and we would play games, hike, and eat lunch at the Park. Tuesdays were bowling, and the children would receive lunch at the bowling alley. On Thursday, we would carpool the children to my home and have a barbecue while swimming in our pool. We made hot dogs and hamburgers on the grill, potato chips and pretzels, and frozen popsicles for dessert. Everyone's favorite day was Wednesday; this was our big trip day. We took the children Storybook Land, Sahara Sam's, Cape May Zoo, Philadelphia Zoo, The Franklin Institute, The Academy of Science, The Wax Museum, Clementon Park, The Funplex, The Aquarium, a ferry ride from Salem, NJ to Pea Pod Island in Delaware, Coco Keys, Red Bank Battlefield, Deptford Skating Rink, and many more. The one trip that stands out in my mind the most is going to Philadelphia to ride the Duck Boats. We went on Wednesday, and the following day, there was a major accident where people lost their lives when a ship hit a duck boat. No more duckboats! I thanked God that night before lying my head on my pillow for the fact that it was not Kamp Kastle Kids the day the Duck Boats Died! This was what you call Serendipity with a Capitol S. Things got even better when Kiddie Korral Kastle was awarded the Best Preschool in Gloucester County. Our school was finally getting recognition for all my hard work and effort. However, I cannot take all the credit because my Assistant Director, "Miss Chrissy," was my right hand, and she contributed a lot to our success. Not to mention my incredible staff, who made my school what it was. Miss Barbara, who had been with me since 1990, and Sheila, affectionately known as MomMom Sheila, were exceptional. Sheila was like a second mother to me and one of the very best. Miss Patty was our 3-year-old teacher; Miss Debbie taught our pre-k; Miss Lynn was our Infant Teacher; and my daughter Erin and Sue, who taught the most difficult class, our toddlers, and my daughter Kristin and Aunt Sis, who operated the before/ after school kids, all of which contributed to making Kiddie Korral Kastle and Kamp Kastle the Great School it was, The Best of Gloucester County!

Time for the Idol

In 2006, my daughter Erin and I went out to San Diego, California, so she could try out for American Idol. Kristin was living there with friends, so we stayed with her. Erin had auditioned twice already, once in New York and once in NJ, but didn't make it. So, we were hoping for the best but prepared for the worst. In any case, it would be a vacation for us, even if she didn't make it. My husband and Chrissy would hold down the school, and we were off for an adventure. It was so exciting when we arrived for the audition that was held at the San Diego Chargers Stadium. The line was unbelievably long. Erin chatted with many people while waiting in line; young artists flocked from all over the country. There had to be 10,000 people all vying to be the next American Idol.

By the time we entered the stadium, we were sunburned and hot! The applicants were corralled into seats, where we would wait for hours until Erin got her chance at stardom. Each person had a number pinned to their outfit. We watched as row after row was taken down to the football field, where ten tables were set up, each with four judges seated around it. When Erin's row got called, I waited in the stadium.

As I sat and watched one contestant after another get ousted, my nerves were rattled. When Erin finally got to the front of the line, I watched her audition but really couldn't hear her. After she was finished, I saw her walk up to the table where the judges were sitting, and I nearly fell off the steps when she turned and held up her Golden Ticket! I was jumping up and down that I really nearly fell. Erin was going to Hollywood! She really has an amazing voice, but I cannot convey the joy and pride I felt when she held up that Golden Ticket. This would mark the second dose of Serendipity in my lifetime.

I met her downstairs, where we had to go into an office. She was handed a contract to sign. She was vowed to secrecy and was not allowed to disclose to anyone that she made it. So, as we left the Stadium, we were overflowing with excitement! We could tell immediate family but no one else, so as we drove back to Kristin's apartment, we had already called every family member; this day was marked as one of the Best.

The Legal Fees Begin

In August of 2006, I received a letter from Mantua Township telling me that my three-year term for the Certificate of Occupancy (CO) for our modular classroom was expiring and that we needed to remove it from the property. The letter said we had received a 3-year temporary C.O., and it was soon expiring. My husband was livid because nowhere on our C.O. does it state temporarily. So, we went to an attorney who would go to court to rectify the issue. However, it was not rectified and the legal fees were rapidly rising. We were granted an extension, but ultimately, we needed to relocate the modular unit and add an extension to the school.

When the house next door went up for auction, we decided to bid on it to secure the property, ensuring there would be no future disputes with a neighboring property owner over the expansion. We won the bid on the property next door to the school and listed our current home on the market. We did not want two mortgages and, soon, three when we bought the school. We found a buyer for our home property, and then were given the bad news from the township on the house on Main St. They were not giving us a certificate of occupancy on the Main St property next to the school. They gave us a list of over $30,000 worth of repairs, including installing a new septic. At the same time, they were running sewer lines down our road. They also insisted on rebuilding the chimney and installing a new heater before issuing a Certificate of Occupancy. But why? What were we supposed to do? Where would we live?

If we sold our homestead, we'd be left without a place to call home. In the end, my husband decided not to accept the buyer's offer, and we took our home off the market. So, we now had to figure out a way to get money to redo the Main St house because our ultimate game plan was to downsize. Kristin was living in San Diego, California, Erin moved to Philadelphia with her boyfriend, and we were down to three children at home. We really did not need 3000 square feet to take care of and the taxes were extremely high! So, for the long term, we wanted to move to Main St. because the idea of having my school right next door to our home would bring so much convenience. We had the Will we now had to find the way.

Kiddie Korral Kastle was once again voted The Best Child-care Center in Gloucester County 2006! Things were going well for the school, with the exception of the township down our throat to move the modular classroom.

Glory Times

By 2007, the school was overflowing with enrollment, our waiting list was long, and financially, we were doing better than ever. The school was voted the "Best of Gloucester County" for the third year in a row. We started making a plan to expand our school; we hired an architect and engineer to assist us. Since we were trying to accommodate the township, they had backed off and let us do so. In the meantime, my Aunt Sis was having health problems and needed help, so she moved into our home and took over our daughter Kristin's room on the first floor that was once our library.

My Assistant Director, Chrissy, moved into Aunt Sis's house with her two children and rented the house. Things were rolling in the right direction; at least, we thought so. But all things considered, with all the commotion of having Aunt Sis to care for and running a school and the mounting legal bills, it was becoming burdensome for both my husband and me. I would go home at lunchtime and fix Aunt Sis's lunch, and before I knew it, I would be running out the door to pick up school-age children from out-of-district schools. I was running like crazy, and our enrollment continued to grow; the Kiddie Korral Kastle was the Most Successful school in the county. The school brought in more than half a million dollars in 2007! If only we had a Crystal ball to have seen what was coming.

The Crash of 2008

We never expected the economy to tank and a recession that tarnished our world in 2008. We began seeing a turn for the worst, parents could not afford to pay their childcare tuition, which caused us to fall behind in our bills at the school. Robbing Peter to pay Paul became a standard we did not need. The poor economics forced us to put a halt to our expansion and just find a way to stay afloat.

Somehow, we managed to get by but by the skin of our teeth. By 2009, business picked up, and we were working for 5 years as voted the Best Childcare Center in Gloucester County. Plus being voted the Best Preschool in South Jersey! Even with the great reputation we had and the enrollment picking up, the legal fees were mounting, and the township was fighting us tooth & nail to try and make us move our school-aged modular classroom; they were determined to use strong-armed tactics to cause us financial stress.

We started a petition online, and our customers fought to keep us in business. It was court hearing after court hearing and money-money-money to the point where we were struggling not only to pay our business bills but our personal bills were also falling behind. Everything was going to hell in a handbasket, and there was absolutely nothing we could do to change the cycle. We just held on holding our breath, awaiting the next court date.

Municipality Manipulation

By June of 2010, we were served with paperwork from Mantua Township Zoning stating that they revoked our C.O. for our Modular Classroom. The summons gave us 1 week to remove the classroom. We hired an attorney to go to court with us to fight this decision. The township kept saying we had a temporary CO and that we failed to move forward with the expansion and addition to our school. Nowhere on our C.O. is there mention of it being temporary! We were being railroaded, and although we did not have the funds to fight this injustice, we had no choice but to fight to save our school. We needed the space in our modular classroom to sustain the school financially. Without the enrollment from that classroom, we would not be able to survive. So, as the legal bills mounted, we were forced to go off the payroll in order to pay the legal bills.

Now, we were literally losing our home to foreclosure and treading water even to pay our utility bills! I could not understand what I ever did to the Township to treat me so unfairly and unjustly. The township sent us a bill for a fine of $5000.00 and proceeded to charge us a $1000.00 fine per day until the modular classroom was removed. The lawyer we hired was in the Township's pocket and did nothing to help us! On January 20, 2011, the township forced my husband to plead guilty of operating without a C.O. in return for the fines to be suspended; however only gave us until September 15, 2011, to move forward with putting an addition on the school and removing the modular classroom.

After running up high legal fees, falling behind in our personal obligations, and not being able to draw a paycheck, we had no ability to move forward with an expansion. My husband found a fantastic lawyer, Mr J. Gable, who filed an appeal with the Superior Court of NJ. This would accomplish two things; first of all, it would allow us to continue to operate in our modular classroom that was currently being used for our summer camp program (Kamp Kastle) that we had filled to capacity and already had taken registration and activity fees for, and two it would give us an opportunity once again save our school. Our personal home was probably going into foreclosure, but my school, which I worked so hard for and had so many years invested in, was worth everything to me. We were facing a do-or-die situation, so if I was going to go down, it would be after fighting with every ounce of strength I had! We were facing an All-or-Nothing scenario. Our customers fully supported us, sending letters to the township on our behalf, and Kiddie Korral Kastle. We also had an online petition with backing from our customers and friends. How could a school that had been running successfully for 25 years! voted the Best in Gloucester County, NJ for 8 years and named the Best Preschool in South Jersey for 6 years, be subjected to such injustice? It's not like we were operating a derogatory business or that we were causing anyone harm. We were a childcare center and preschool offering our parents exemplary care and education. It just blows my mind, and if I'm being honest, it is hurting the wonderful staff, as well as the working parents that have entrusted our service to care for their most prized possessions, "their children."

On April 3, 2013, my husband went to Superior Court in Atlantic City, NJ, where it was determined that Mantua Township Zoning Board could not prove my husband willingly pleaded guilty of not having a valid C.O., therefore all fines were ruled unjust and uncollectible, the Superior Court ruled in our favor. Thank God we received a winning day in court. I thanked God for this blessing as I laid my head to rest that night. Isn't it funny that on my oldest daughter's 32nd birthday, we came out victorious, another serendipity moment!

Superior Court Ruling on April 3, 2013

James E. Gabel, attorney for appellants. Richardson, Galella & Austermuhl, attorneys for respondent State of New Jersey/Township of Mantua (Linda A. Galella, on the brief).

In this appeal, defendant Harry K. Frye 1 challenges the establishment of the factual basis upon which he entered a conditional guilty plea for violating a municipal ordinance. After a careful review of the record evidence, we determined a valid plea was not entered. Accordingly, we vacate the conviction and reverse.

156

The facts surrounding this matter are set forth in the Law Division judge's April 3, 2013 written opinion.

The Fryes obtained a Certificate of Occupancy for the trailer from the Mantua Township Zoning Board in 2003 with the understanding that the trailer was to serve as a temporary classroom while the owners received site plan approval from the Zoning Board for an expansion of the existing daycare facility. The owners received preliminary site plan approval for the construction project on June 8, 2007. In that approval, the Zoning Board stated that final site plan approval would be contingent upon the removal of the temporary trailer. Subsequently, the owners were unable to obtain the financing needed to continue with the construction project. The trailer remained on the property and continued to be used as a classroom.

The Certificate of Occupancy for the trailer was revoked on June 2, 2010. Subsequently, the owners received several summonses for, among other things, occupancy following the revocation of a certificate of occupancy. Defendant Harry K. Frye appeared in Mantua Township Municipal Court on January 20, 2011, to address the summonses. He was represented by counsel and entered a conditional guilty plea. It was represented that Brian D. Lozuke, Esquire represented the defendant and had discussed the removal of the trailer with the defendant over "many months." The terms of the conditional guilty plea required that the defendant proceed in good faith with an application for final site plan approval and then proceed with the construction project. It was agreed that "under no circumstances will the defendant be permitted to maintain the trailer which exists at the site beyond September 15, 2011." A $5,000 fine was suspended, and if the trailer remained after that date, the $5,000 fine would be due, and an additional fine of $1,000 per day would accrue for every day the trailer remained on the property after the date agreed upon for removal.

The defendant did not remove the trailer by September 15. As a result, he was summoned to appear before the Mantua Township Municipal Court on July 12, 2012. At the hearing, the judge determined that the defendant violated the terms of the January

20, 2011, conditional plea and imposed a $5000 fine and a $301,000 fine, representing the $1000 per day penalty. The defendant appealed from the July 12, 2012, municipal court disposition and the imposition of the fines and penalties.

The matter went before a Law Division judge for a de novo trial on January 18, 2013. Initially, the court decided to limit the appeal to a review of the record of the July 12, 2012 proceeding imposing the fines. However, the defense counsel persuasively argued the judge could not properly consider the imposition of the sentence without reviewing the plea, which arguably lacked a factual basis. The court agreed and determined that "there may be no basis for the imposition of the fines if the plea underlying that was not properly done. And although time has run to appeal [,] . I have to consider that issue."

The judge invited counsel to submit a written argument on whether there was a factual basis for the defendant's conditional guilty plea and whether the plea was voluntarily given. In his April 3, 2013, written decision, the judge found that an adequate factual basis had been established, and the defendant entered into the conditional plea freely, voluntarily, knowingly, and without coercion. The judge further found defendant violated the terms and conditions of the plea agreement and, thereafter, imposed a $5000 fine. As for the $1000 accumulating fine, the court found $301,000 to be unreasonable in light of the municipality's delay in filing the violation notice. The judge vacated that portion of the fine and remanded for further consideration of an appropriate per diem penalty.

This appeal followed, where the defendant raised the following arguments:

I. THE ZONING PERMIT ISSUED TO THE KIDDIE KORRAL KASTLE/DANA FRYE ON JUNE 3, 2003 WAS A USE PERMITTED BY ORDINANCE.

II. THE CERTIFICATE OF OCCUPANCY ISSUED TO APPELLANT HARRY K. FRYE ON NOVEMBER 5, 2003, FOR THE TRAILER (ACTUALLY A CUSTOM-MADE

"CUSTOM MODULAR CLASSROOM") WAS ISSUED WITH-
OUT CONDITIONS AND WAS NOT A TEMPORARY CER-
TIFICATE OF OCCUPANCY.

III. PRELIMINARY SITE PLAN APPROVAL WAS
GRANTED TO THE APPELLANTS ON FEBRUARY 19, 2008
AND MEMORIALIZED, PURSUANT TO RESOLUTION 08–
15 OF THE MANTUA TOWNSHIP PLANNING BOARD.

IV. THE JUNE 2, 2010 LETTER FROM TED BAN-
FORD, THE MANTUA TOWNSHIP ZONING OFFICER, PUR-
PORTING TO REVOKE THE CERTIFICATE OF OCCU-
PANCY IN ERROR FOR THE TRAILER/" CUSTOMIZED
MODULAR CLASSROOM" WAS INEFFECTIVE AND UN-
LAWFUL FOR A VARIETY OF REASONS.

V. AS INDICATED IN THE COURT'S OPINION, AF-
TER HEARING THE ARGUMENTS OF COUNSEL ON JAN-
UARY 18, 2013, IT WAS DECIDED THAT A DETERMINA-
TION MUST BE MADE AS TO WHETHER AN ADEQUATE
FACTUAL BASIS WAS PLACED ON THE RECORD AND
WHETHER THE DEFENDANT ACTED KNOWINGLY AND
VOLUNTARILY WHEN HE ENTERED INTO THE GUILTY
PLEA ON JANUARY 20, 2011. FURTHER SUBMISSIONS
WERE TO BE PROVIDED TO THE COURT AND RE-
VIEWED.

IT IS THE APPELLANTS' POSITION THAT THERE WAS
NEVER A FACTUAL BASIS PLACED UPON THE RECORD,
NOR WAS THE "CONDITIONAL" PLEA ENTERED INTO
BY THE APPELLANT KNOWINGLY AND VOLUNTARILY;
THEREFORE, THE SAME IS SUBJECT TO REVIEW AND
POSSIBLE MODIFICATION OR REJECTION BY THIS
COURT.

VI. IN ACCORDANCE WITH THE "CONDITIONAL
PLEA" OF JANUARY 20, 2011, WHICH IS CONTESTED
HEREIN, THE APPELLANTS DID APPLY FOR FINAL SITE
PLAN APPROVAL BEFORE THE MANTUA TOWNSHIP
PLANNING BOARD. SAID FINAL SITE PLAN APPROVAL

WAS GRANTED PURSUANT TO MANTUA TOWNSHIP PLANNING BOARD RESOLUTION 11–13 ON APRIL 19, 2011.

VII.   THE FINES AND COSTS IMPOSED BY THE MUNICIPAL COURT EXCEEDED THE STATUTORY AUTHORITY GIVEN TO MUNICIPAL COURTS IN FIXING FINES, PENALTIES AND COSTS BY A MUNICIPAL COURT IN THE STATE OF NEW JERSEY.

We have reviewed the record as well as the defendant's arguments and conclude that in light of our conclusion that the defendant's conditional guilty plea must be vacated, we need not address Points I through IV, Point VI, and Point VII. We take no position as to whether Points I through IV and Point VI, as the Law Division found, are issues that should have been presented to the planning board and, if not resolved to the defendant's satisfaction, raised in an action in lieu of prerogative writs. We, therefore, limit our discussion to Point V.

On an appeal such as this, we "consider only the action of the Law Division and not that of the municipal court," State v. Oliveri, 336 N.J.Super. 244, 251 (App.Div.2001), because the Law Division's determination is de novo on the record from the municipal court. R. 3:23–8(a). Our review of purely legal issues is plenary. State v. Goodman, 415 N.J.Super. 210, 225 (App.Div.2010), certif. denied, 205 N.J. 78 (2011). We are limited to determining whether the Law Division's de novo factual findings "could reasonably have been reached on sufficient credible evidence present in the record." State v. Johnson,42 N.J. 146, 162.

To review the lower court's assessment of the defendant's conditional plea, we start with the premise that proceedings in municipal courts prosecuting violations of municipal ordinances are essentially criminal in nature. State v. Barnes, 168 N.J.Super. 311, 314 (App.Div.1979) (citing State v. Yaccarino, 3 N.J. 291, 295 (1949)). Consequently, the judge taking a plea to a violation of a municipal ordinance must satisfy the same requirements for taking a guilty plea as an offense governed by our criminal code. See

State v. Stafford, 365 N.J.Super. 6, 11, 14 (App.Div.2003) (noting that although the defendant was charged with violating municipal ordinances, "the practice mandated in the New Jersey Criminal Code . should also be followed" and guilt "must be established beyond a reasonable doubt"); see also State v. Martin, 335 N.J.Super. 447, 450–51 (App.Div.2000) (reiterating the necessity to ensure the voluntariness of a defendant's plea as well as the consequences of the plea).

It is clear that for a plea of guilty to be accepted, there must be a factual basis for the plea. State v. Smullen, 118 N.J. 408, 414 (1990). A "factual basis for a guilty plea must obviously include defendant's admission of guilt of the [offense] or the acknowledgment of facts constituting the essential elements of the [offense]." State v. Pineiro, 385 N.J.Super. 129, 137 (App.Div.2006) (quoting State v. Sainz, 107 N.J. 283, 293 (1987)). A judge must be "satisfied from the lips of the defendant that he committed the acts which constitute the [offense]." State v. Slater, 198 N.J. 145, 155 (2009). Therefore, "[e]ven if a defendant wished to plead guilty to [an offense] he or she did not commit, he or she may not do so. No court may accept such a plea." Smullen, supra, 118 N.J. at 415. "The need to establish a sufficient factual basis for a guilty plea is not obviated by the fact that the plea is part of a negotiated plea agreement." Sainz, supra, 107 N.J. at 293; see also State v. Butler, 89 N.J. 220, 224–25 .

In reviewing a trial court's decision on a motion to vacate a plea, we will reverse only if the decision is "clearly erroneous." State v. Mustaro, 411 N.J.Super. 91, 99 (App.Div.2009). To resolve the motion, the court must consider the following factors: (1) whether the defendant has asserted a colorable claim of innocence; (2) the nature and strength of the defendant's reasons for withdrawal of the plea; (3) whether the plea was entered as part of a plea bargain; and (4) whether withdrawal of the plea would result in unfair prejudice to the State or unfair advantage to the accused. Slater, supra, 198 N.J. at 158–61.

We recite the relevant portion of the January 20, 2011, plea hearing to put the defendant's claim in its proper context. As noted above, the defendant was charged with violating Municipal Ordinance 230–92(a)(3) for continuing "the use of [a] temporary trailer without [an] issued construction permit" after the revocation of the Certificate of Occupancy (CO) by the Zoning officer. The following individuals appeared in the municipal court proceeding: the defendant with his attorney, Brian Lozuke; Kelly Conroy, the Municipal Prosecutor; and Samuel Ragonese, the municipal planning board solicitor, who served as special prosecutor for the State. The municipal court judge reviewed the negotiated plea agreement that called for the defendant to enter a conditional guilty plea to a violation of Municipal Ordinance 230–92(a)(3), "occupancy beyond the date by which the Zoning officer of this town revoked a Certificate of Occupancy."

After the judge recited the agreement, he asked the defendant,

Court: Is that correct? Sir, do you understand that?"

Defendant: Yeah, I understand what was said.

Court: Do you agree to this?

Defendant: Not entirely

Court: What is it that you don't agree to?

Defendant: The guilty plea on the particular summons for operating without a CO. I have a CO.

The defendant continued to question whether there should be a guilty plea or a fine. Mr. Ragonese conducted the colloquy with respect to the defendant's understanding of the settlement and voluntariness of his plea:

Mr. Ragonese: Mr. Frye, you have been represented in this matter throughout by Mr. Lozuke; is that correct?

A Correct.

Q   And you understand that the terms of the settlement require you to file an application with the Mantua Township Planning Board by March 10, 2011, seeking final site plan approval for an addition, should you choose to proceed; is that correct?

A Correct.

Q And, you understand that if you proceed and obtain final site plan approval, you must obtain a building permit from the Township of Mantua by June 1, correct?

A Correct.

Q And, that under no circumstances shall the trailer on-site remain there beyond September 15; right?

A I have a question for you.

Q No, just answer my questions, okay? I'm asking the questions. So, do you understand or do you not that the trailer must be removed by September 15 under all circumstances?

A Yes, I understand.

Q Okay. Now, do you understand that if you do not meet any one of those three benchmark dates, the town will be entitled to hold you in contempt for failure to make payment of the $5000 fine and to also seek the imposition of an additional fine of $1000 per day for each day of noncompliance with the terms of this conditional plea? Do you understand that?

A Right, that's what we talked about earlier that I was questioning.

Q Right. So, do you understand the terms of the settlement in full; correct?

A Correct.

Q All right. Now, you're not presently under the influence of any medications, correct?

A Correct.

Q You don't take any medications that would affect your ability to exercise clear judgment in deciding what to do in this case; correct?

A Correct.

Q And, today you have entered into this conditional plea freely and voluntarily, correct?

163

A Yeah, I have no choice.

Q   And, in making this decision to accept the conditional plea, you decided that you could have gone to trial and tried this case; you're aware of that, right?

A Yeah, my attorney advised me that we should make a resolution.

Q   And, you have agreed to make a resolution; correct?

A Yes, we're doing so now.

Q   And, you understand that the terms of this conditional plea are in the place of a guilty finding or a finding of not guilty. Do you understand that?

A No, now I'm confused about what you just said.

Q   Okay. What we're doing here today replaces a trial and a finding of guilt or not guilt. Do you understand that?

A Right.

Q   Okay. And you're entering this plea after having received the advice that you just referred to by your counsel, right?

A Right.

Q   And, you've had an opportunity to speak to Mr. Lozuke at length about this case?

A Correct.

Q   Over many months now, right?

A Correct.

Q   And, you're reaching this—and you've reached this plea today with your own free accord, correct?

A Correct.

Q   Do you understand that the other charges will be held in abeyance, and so long as you comply with the terms of the conditional plea, they will be dismissed? Do you understand that?

A I thought they were dismissed.

Q   No, they will be dismissed if you comply with the terms of the benchmarks that we've established; otherwise, you could be subject to prosecution. Do you understand that now?

A I don't necessarily agree.

THE COURT: [W]hat I have marked . is that I am holding these three remaining charges with the intent to dismiss on full compliance, and ultimately, if there is full compliance, all charges will be dismissed.

MR. FRYE: Well, what I don't understand, Your Honor, is [Ragonese] said that I'm entering—I'm not entering a guilty or a not guilty plea today, but yet there's one particular summons that you're stating that I am guilty of if I do not make the terms of the three dates that will be prosecuted.

THE COURT: No, that's—essentially, that's correct; under summons # 005908, I have marked—

MR. FRYE: So, that means I am entering a guilty plea of that and [Ragonese] said I'm not.

THE COURT: —and I marked it "conditional."

MR. LOZUKE: Okay. It means that provided there's full compliance, it will be dismissed, as well as the other charges.

THE COURT: All right. It is a provisional or conditional plea, and if you comply with what you've agreed to, this conditional or provisional plea of guilty will be marked "dismissed."

MR. FRYE: I understand, Your Honor. I—

THE COURT: The other three charges, I have not marked any plea to—

MR. FRYE: Okay.

THE COURT: Okay, other than a plea of not guilty, and with the—and I marked it "hold" with the intent to dismiss on condition of compliance with the requirements under this summons.

MR. FRYE: And, that particular summons, what does that state again what the charges are?

165

THE COURT: That's a summons, continued use of a trailer without a Certificate of Occupancy in violation of Local Ordinance # 230–92(a)(3).

MR. FRYE: But, Your Honor, that's what I'm saying is I do have a CO—a current CO presently.

MR. LOZUKE: But, that is what is being disputed. The charge will be dismissed upon compliance with the settlement agreement.

MR. FRYE: Well, I understand, but what I'm saying is, how can I plead guilty to something that I know that I have?

MR. LOZUKE: That is what is in dispute, and that is already resolved. So, that charge will be dismissed along with the other three upon compliance with the terms that were just read.

MR. FRYE: All right, I have no choice.

MR. CONROY: Your Honor, —

MR. RAGONESE: If I could just follow along, Your Honor.

THE COURT: Yes.

BY MR. RAGONESE:

Q   You are aware that you received a certified letter revoking the CO; correct?

A Yeah, I did receive a letter, yes.

Q   And, you are aware that the charge for occupying without the CO followed the revocation of that earlier CO . by certified letter. Do you recall that, right?

A Yeah. But what was the reason why . revocation was set?

Q   Well, the letter explains that it was revoked, and your attorney has explained to you that trailers are not allowed generally, correct?

A Yes, . it's a nonconformity.

Q   Now, also sir, today I would like to ask you, has anyone offered to pay you money to make this plea?

A Offered to pay me money?

Q Yes.

A No.

Q Have you been offered anything of value to enter into this plea?

A No.

Q Have you been forced or threatened with harm in any way to make this conditional plea of guilty? Yes, or no?

A. No.

MR. RAGONESE: I have nothing further, Your Honor.

BY MR. RAGONESE:

Q Last—one last question. Are you satisfied with the services of Mr. Lozuke and his office?

A Absolutely.

[(Emphasis added).]

As stated above, the defendant appealed from the order of July 2012, in which the court imposed a financial penalty. The defendant did not appeal the January 2011 conviction for violating the ordinance. Yet at the trial de novo, the judge, sua sponte, found it necessary to review the sufficiency of the defendant's plea as a preliminary matter to review the propriety of the fines and penalties imposed. The judge found the plea to be sufficient to establish a violation of the Municipal Ordinance. However, we cannot accept that ruling when the plain reading of the transcript lays bare the defendant's confusion with respect to the possession of the CO, an essential element of the offense.

The subsequent efforts by the court and counsel to salvage the plea were unavailing. The defendant's eventual acknowledgment of his understanding of the negotiated plea agreement is not tantamount to establishing a factual basis for the plea. See Sainz, supra, 107 N.J. at 293. ("The need to establish a sufficient factual basis for a guilty plea is not obviated by the fact that the plea is part of a negotiated plea agreement.") We discern that the defendant understood the plea agreement; namely, he had to apply for final site plan approvals in March 2011 to receive a construction permit by June 2011 and remove the temporary trailer by September 15, 2011. However, when the defendant attempted to inform the court about his possession of a certificate of occupancy (CO) and other exculpatory evidence, opposing counsel prevented him from speaking. The record clearly shows that the defendant did not understand how he could be found guilty of having a trailer on the property "after the revocation of a certificate of occupancy." In order to have established a factual basis, the defendant must have admitted to guilt of all the essential elements of the offense. In our view, the defendant did not do so here.

While we understand the municipality's goal is to have the defendant remove the "temporary" trailer that has been on the defendant's property from 2003 up to the present day, the record does not satisfy us that the defendant acknowledged the essential criteria of a guilty plea: "that the defendant is, in fact, guilty of the [offense] for which he is being sentenced." Id. at 292. Unlike many defendants who, in their plea colloquy, may provide only stilted, monosyllabic responses to counsel's and the court's questions, here, the defendant's responses are sufficiently clear to convince us that his plea lacks the requisite voluntariness and acknowledgment of guilt.

Consequently, we vacate the defendant's guilty plea and the sentence imposed. We remand the matter to the Mantua Township Municipal Court for trial or further proceedings. Martin, supra, 335 N.J.Super. at 452.

Reverse and remanded. We do not retain jurisdiction.

FOOTNOTES

FN1. Defendant Dana Frye did not participate in this appeal. Therefore, reference to the defendant pertains solely to Harry K. Frye. FN1. Defendant Dana Frye did not participate in this appeal. Therefore, reference to the defendant pertains solely to Harry K. Frye.

FN2. The summons references an incorrect Ordinance section number, Ordinance 230–55, rather than 230–92(a)(3). The parties acknowledged the error below. FN2. The summons references an incorrect Ordinance section number, Ordinance 230–55, rather than 230–92(a)(3). The parties acknowledged the error below.

PER CURIAM

When it Rains it Pours!

We had so many problems, but nothing to compare to this when I was handed the fate and excruciating pain of losing my Dear Father on April 10, 2012! My Dad was in Lady of Lourdes Hospital recovering from a heart attack, the same hospital in which I was born. It was on a Tuesday, only two days after Easter Sunday. I can't tell you how I made it to the hospital in one piece, but when my mother called me to tell me I needed to get to the hospital because my father took a turn for the worse, I drove like a bat at of hell down 130 to get there.

When I arrived, my mother was sitting in a wheelchair in a room outside of the intensive care unit, with a nurse holding her hand. The nurse explained they were working on my father, but it didn't look good. When the doctor came out and said they did all they could, but he didn't make it, my mother insisted on seeing him. As soon as she entered the room, she started crying hysterically and was screaming at the doctor, saying she didn't get to say Goodbye! Upon getting up out of the wheelchair, she began shaking all over, and then her eyes rolled back in her head, and the nurses grabbed her before she collapsed on the floor.

By this time, I was screaming and crying because I thought my mother was having a stroke! The nurse informed me she was having a seizure, and they put her on a gurney and wheeled her out of the room to an intensive care unit to be seen by a doctor. I can remember sitting on the floor in the hallway crying, left all by myself, feeling totally lost and beyond upset; I was mortified! Trying to process that I just lost my father, and worried that I may lose my mother too! It was more than I could bear when I saw my sister Kelly and her husband Curt, followed by my two oldest daughters and my husband, running up the hallway toward me.

As I hugged my sister, balling my eyes out, it was comforting to know I was no longer alone, and as we held each other tight, we cried for the loss of our father and prayed for our mother. It would be hours before we would learn that our Mother suffered a Grand

Mal seizure and was admitted to the hospital. We were not permitted to see her until 9:00 pm that night, and although she was sedated, she was still crying when we entered her room. She kept saying that she couldn't live without our father, and we knew that this was going to be the most crippling time for our family. It would be over 5 days before my mother would be released from the hospital, and we would start planning my father's funeral.

It was a warm and bright sunny day on April 16th, 2012, when our family would say our last goodbyes to the Great Man I called "Dad." My daughter Erin sang "Amazing Grace" at the funeral, and I'm not sure how she was able to pull it off, but she did it beautifully with her amazing voice. The days after the funeral were very dark as my mother went into a deep depression in which no one seemed able to help her. My daughter Kristin and her boyfriend Joe moved in with her so she wouldn't be alone. Eventually, she began to come around, but 2012 will always be one of the darkest and saddest years for our family. It was compounded in July of 2012 when my husband's father would pass away, too. So, both my husband and I would lose our fathers in the same year, merely 3 months apart. Murphy's Law was lethal in 2012!

Do Or Die

On April 3, 2013, my husband went to Superior Court in Atlantic City, NJ, where it was determined that Mantua Township Zoning Board could not prove my husband willingly pleaded guilty of not having a valid C.O., therefore all fines were ruled unjust and uncollectible, the Superior Court ruled in our favor. Thank God we received a winning day in court. I thanked God for this blessing as I laid my head to rest that night. Isn't it funny that on my oldest daughter's 32nd birthday, we came out victorious, another serendipity moment

Shower Underway

My oldest daughter is having a baby and I planned her shower in NJ with the help of my assistant Director. The theme is based on one of her favorite fairytales, "Alice in Wonderland." It was being held at Valley Caterer's Hall because a dear friend of mine owned it, and I was certain it would be a wonderful choice to honor my daughter. As expected, the food was delicious, and the party was perfect. My daughter received so many wonderful gifts, and everything turned out beautifully; the only issue we had to deal with was shipping all her gifts to San Francisco, California, where she was living. In 2 months, I would be flying out to be there for the birth of my 1st grandchild. Exciting times were on the horizon.

Summer camp enrollment was filled to capacity, and I was just bussing with happiness. On June 14th, my husband drove me to the airport for my flight to San Francisco, where I planned to be present for the birth of my grandchild. Kristin's due date was June 17th, though it seemed likely she might deliver later, as I had experienced with her. I hoped she would not have to go through the lengthy labor I had endured during her birth. I accompanied her to a visit to her obstetrician on the 15th of June, where the Dr told her she was just beginning to dilate and that it could be any-time. The Dr also said it just depends when she's ready to arrive. Kristin, not wanting to know what the sex of her baby was, and had made that known from day one, sat up on the table and very loudly said! "You did not just tell me the sex of my baby"!!! The Dr., realizing that she fumbled, said, "no, I always refer to babies as she." Kristin was so sure she was carrying a boy, and in fact bought a lot of boy's clothing, left bewildered. The seventeenth came and went, and no baby. Finally, on June 27th, she woke up with back pain, and by 5:00 PM that evening, Joe (her husband) took her to the hospital. My daughter Erin and I went to grab din-ner before going to the hospital. As we ate, I said to Erin, this is so ironic because I went to the hospital in labor with Kristin at 5:00 PM on April 1st, and she was not born until April 3rd at 3:04 AM. I hope this is not going to be a sign of a repeat of her birth. When we arrived at the hospital, Kristin was only 2 centimeters dilated, which was exactly the same scenario with me. By 11:00 AM on the 28th, Kristin decided she needed to stop the pain and received an epidural to relieve the agony. I was glad she had a Dr.

sympathetic to her needs because the Dr. I had for her delivery was not willing to give me anything for the pain, a big advocate of natural childbirth, and I despised him for it. By midnight on the 29th, Kristin's Dr. said she was dilated eight centimeters, and hopefully, the baby would be born soon. Kristin kept wanting to push as she felt so much pressure; she was shaking from low blood pressure, and I was starting to panic! The Dr gave her something in her IV to bring her pressure up, and by 2:52 AM, she was able to start pushing. As I held one leg and Erin held the other, Joe videotaped at the foot of the bed; I said your baby might be born at the same time you were if you push hard. As it turned out, we welcomed a Big, Beautiful, Bouncing Baby girl at 3:12 AM. She was alert with her Beautiful blue eyes wide open and looking around. She weighed 9lbs,12 ozs. She was 22 inches long; she had big blue eyes and blonde hair. She barely fit in the baby bassinet, and she really looked like a two. Month-old baby. She was perfect! Welcome to the world, "Margaux Katherine." So, Kristin's labor began at the same time as mine but took 8 minutes longer than mine did with her. Perhaps genetics are stronger than what we think. Or is it just to be chalked up to another serendipity added to our family tree?

Tough Times

I should be happy, but instead, I'm sick again. The turmoil of the fight to save my school has worn me. After returning home from California, I found that our financial situation had gotten worse, which caused a riff in my marriage as well as my well-being. Peter has no money to pay Paul; the bank has started foreclosure on our home! When will our lives return to normal? What was going on? By 2014, all hell broke out! It started out with telephone lines ringing in my bedroom but it was not our house phone nor my cell phone! I started finding jacks behind furniture that were ringing without a phone. I would go to my school, and I would be greeted with someone talking to me through my security cameras! This, I know, sounds crazy, but it's truly the truth. It kept getting worse, and of course, my investigating skills became the top priority to the bane of my existence. I was being told that my husband was running porn online from my school. This was not going to continue, so I began troubleshooting, which eventually led to finding 75 ethernet cable wires behind a wall in my 4-year-old classroom.

My husband told me if I didn't stop investigating, he would shut my school down. This literally began the War of the Roses! I moved out of the home that we were losing and took my daughter Nadia with me. I purchased two sleeping matts, where Nadia and I would sleep on the floor at my school. My husband no longer worked at the school, which left me to carry the entire burden. What made things worse was the money situation. By the end of the summer, things could not have been worse! My assistant Director quit, which would mean more on my plate to continue running my school. It was impossible for me to handle a job that previously required three people to complete.

Following a recommendation from my church, I hired a tech-savvy individual to assist, as I lacked computer skills. In fact, I had reverted to using paper records to manage tuition, expenses, and bills. Eventually, I found myself unable to use the computer at all. It was passcode protected with a password I did not know.

Somehow, someway, someone remotely changed the master password! I struggled the best I could to stay afloat, but in January 2015, an African American woman showed up at my school saying she was from Institutional Abuse and said a parent accused me of child abuse and told me I needed to leave the school. This woman looked very familiar to me; however, I could not place her at the time. She told me who the woman was who accused me of this awful accusation, and she was a friend of my daughters! As God is my witness, I would Never Ever abuse any child in my school! I never even physically punished my own children! This was a vicious lie! On January 29th, 2015, three women came out to the school.

One was a gal I'd call Jen, who said she was from NJ State Licensing and was taking over as my license inspector; when I asked where is Calista, who has been my inspector for years? She answered - "I'm taking over, that's all." She asked me if I recognized her. And then it dawned on me that she was a friend of my daughter's and actually spent the night in our home! There was another African American woman who said she was there because someone accused me of doing drugs and that she was told I was abusing drugs! So now I'm being accused of child abuse and being a drug addict! I explained that I was given pain medication through a doctor for a chronic illness and that I was not even taking the medication anymore. When My husband left the school, I stopped taking the pain meds because I had to transport children.

Nothing I said mattered, and I was told I had to appoint an employee in charge and leave the school immediately! I was also told I was not allowed at my school for any reason; even after hours, I could not return. They also took my 171/2-year-old daughter to my mother's house, and I was told I could have no contact with her! As I left the school, it was snowing and freezing cold. I had no place to go, very little money, and our home that was in foreclosure had no electricity or gas turned on, so it was freezing cold! As I sat in a parking lot drinking coffee to warm up, I broke down hysterically crying! I called Mary, my birth mother, and cried my eyes out to her. She asked me to come to St Louis

175

and stay with her, but I didn't have money to even get a motel room for the night, let alone buy a plane ticket! I ended up sitting in the WaWa parking lot for hours. At least if I got too cold, I could go in and get warmed up. It was dark, freezing cold, and snowing like a blizzard when my husband pulled next to me in the parking lot. He knew what had happened by one of my employees calling him. He told me to come back to the house with him. When we entered the home, I was shocked by what I saw! The house was ransacked; as I looked down the hallway, there was a clear plastic stapled to the ceiling all around the family room. The ceiling in the kitchen was partially caved in, and the beautiful oriental carpet in our family room was covered with wood debris and pieces of sheet rock that fell from the ceiling. The house reeked from mold!

My Prince Charming, who reminded me of Jeremiah Johnson at first sight, was now living like him. He proceeded to put logs in our fireplace to warm the room. He reorganized our pit set to form a bed. He went upstairs to grab blankets from our bed, and within 30 minutes, we were wrapped up like cocoons and fast asleep. When I woke in the morning, I was so sick, coughing my head off and burning up with a fever! I went to my Dr, who gave me antibiotics and cough medicine and sent me for a chest x-ray.

Later that day, it was confirmed that I had pneumonia. Sleeping in our moldy, cold house was not an option. My husband got us a motel room in Williamstown, NJ, where we stayed for one night. The next day, we went to this awful motel in Gibbstown that was once the beautiful Dutch Inn and is where my birth mother and aunt stayed upon coming to NJ to meet me. It was now called the Ramada Inn, and the place was nasty, with blood-stained carpets in the hallway. Harry was working selling construction jobs in central NJ, so while he worked all day, I sat in this disgusting motel room waiting for a court date to end this traumatic nightmare. This has to be the lowest point in my entire life! Within a week, I had hired an attorney from a referral from my church and was in court. I entered the courtroom believing I was defending myself from being accused of child abuse, but I quickly learned that the child abuse accusation was off the table, and I was being ordered to go for drug testing because it was believed I was abusing drugs. I was appalled because I had never abused drugs; I basically had a prescription for 5 mg. Tablets of hydrocodone, which I took twice a day until a Dr Burger put me on methadone because she said that it was a man-made pain medication that would not damage my liver. I didn't question her, nor did I investigate to find out what it was. Had I known it was used to wean a person off of opiates such as hydrocodone, perhaps the event would have gone smoothly.

I was prescribed to take one methadone in the morning, one hydrocodone mid-day, and another methadone pill at night. I just took 1 methadone in the morning and occasionally one at night but skipped the hydrocodone mid-day. I had a business to operate and didn't want to feel drugged. So, never did I abuse drugs; I was very cautious, and in fact wouldn't even have a glass of wine or a beer when I took these medications. The judge ordered me to go for drug testing twice a week at a place called SODAT. The Judge explained I would receive a call to go get tested, and I had only hours to get there, or it would be marked as a failed test.

Anyone who knew me clearly understood that I'm a rule follower and that I was bound and determined to prove to the judge, as well as the world, that I was not taking or abusing drugs! In February, my husband and I moved into an apartment on the 3rd floor, within a mile of my school. The school in which I was ordered not to step foot in! I couldn't go there and partake in any duties, pay the bills, pick up my mail, absolutely nothing! The calls would begin to come to my cell phone by the end of February to be tested. I would drop whatever I was doing and get there within an hour's time. I was drowning in sadness; I missed my daughter, who I was also banned from seeing!

When I tell you that the way I was being treated when I went for this drug testing is inhumane. I was treated as if I were a criminal! They would make me sit in a waiting room for what seemed like an hour or more. Then, they would make me sign a paper agreeing to the testing and forget about having any dignity or pride left. A woman would accompany me in the bathroom, tell me to drop my pants and pee in this cup, and she would oversee to watch and listen while I urinated in this cup! Talk about losing every ounce of privacy, freedom, and civil rights! Believe me when I tell you that you have never experienced a low so demeaning until you become court-ordered for drug testing. This process would continue for 24 days until I would be back in court to learn my fate.

As I said, I was not taking drugs, and that was exactly what was determined after a little over three weeks of sheer Hell. However, one of the African American women who came out to my school, who turned out to be working for the Drug and Alcohol substance abuse organization, argued in court that I must be crazy if no opiates or alcohol were in my system because I believed things were happening that were not. I tried to speak to defend myself, and my lawyer stopped me. So now I was being ordered to have psychological testing. What in the world was happening to me? I prayed to God that this whole ordeal would end! How did this happen to me? I began feeling very depressed because I had absolutely no control over my life. Rumors began to spread that I was kicked out of my school for abusing a child! As everyone knows, it only takes one person to start a rumor, and from there, it's like a wildfire without water to extinguish! In mid-March, I went to a building that was aligned with security guards inside. I had to sign in and wait for my number to be called.

As I made my way down this very long hallway, I was taken into a room where they questioned me and took notes of my answers. They kept asking me if I wanted to hurt myself. Then they asked me if I wanted to kill myself. That was enough for me, I barked back...." No, I don't want to kill myself. I'm not suicidal, and I feel as if I'm being treated unfairly!" After that little outburst, I was escorted to another room and handed a test with many crazy questions on it. Having had an educational background in nursing, I was fully aware of what all my answers should be and completed the test in 20 minutes. As I was dismissed, all I knew was I couldn't get out of there fast enough. By March end, my mother had a knee that needed surgery, and my daughter, who was almost 18 at the time, was put in foster care with a woman in Clayton, NJ, who had other teenagers of mothers in the court system also. She shared a bedroom with a teen girl who smoked cigarettes and Marijuana every day. They were being dropped off in Glassboro, NJ, where they were basically free to run the streets for hours at a time. How the courts deemed this better or safer for my daughter than with her parents, who loved her, is beyond my comprehension.

We were supposed to go back to court at the beginning of April, but that was postponed until May. Murphy's Law bit me again. As I was sitting watching television one night, a commercial came on for Apple, and lo and behold, there was my Institutional Abuse Inspector on television selling Apple products! So, she was an actress, apparently hired to accuse me of child abuse! The kettle keeps getting blacker.

"You Can't Fight City Hall."

So, as the saying goes, in the end, City Hall Always Wins. On April 22, 2015, only 83 days after I was banished from my school, the township's Fire Inspector came out and closed my school. The reason for the written summons was that because my phone bill failed to be paid, they shut my phone service off, which shut my Fire and Security System down. Therefore, having reason to close the school.

The summons had no court date, no rebuttal, and no way to fight the action. Just like that, Kiddie Korral Kastle's doors were closed forever! I cried for days, which turned into weeks. My hard work to create a great school for so many families and wonderful children was gone, and I was defeated! Ten years voted the Best Childcare Center in Gloucester County, and eight years voted the Best Preschool in South Jersey was over! The only thing I had left to fight for was getting my daughter home and finding a way to survive. Although my husband was working for a construction company, we were literally behind the eight ball. We were slowly sinking faster than quicksand.

By mid-May, we were back in court for the final time. My lawyer kept telling me I had to go into the courtroom and say I was a family in need in order to get my daughter home. I didn't want to do it because I felt as if I was never a family in need. I always worked and provided for everyone. I donated money weekly to my church, I donated computers to the local school, and I employed 14-17 employees for years! I taught Catholic Catechism for 2nd grade for 6 years at my church. I was not a slacker in any way, shape or form. I felt violated by false accusations, and now I was going to be labeled a family in need! The lawyer explained that this is how it had to be in order for my daughter to come home. After being manipulated and coaxed, I finally did what I had to do. My daughter was released to come home with my husband and me only 23 days before her 18th birthday. In hindsight, she would have been free to come home on her own will at 18 years old. What I did learn in court that day was that besides having no opiates in my body from the testing I had to do, someone came into our home and took over 1000 hydrocodone pills that were hidden behind my jewelry in a hidden compartment that was not visible without opening a wooden door. My husband is the only person who knew where the medication was hidden. The judge made a comment that had I have been taking or abusing this medication; there would not have been 1000+ pills left in my home. I was accused, tried, and hung without a fair trial, and now I was left to find a way to survive. My daughter finished her junior year in High School while living in the apartment on the 3rd floor with us. Thank God for that.

For her 18th birthday my husband gave her a 1993 Hyundai Tiburon, which we put a big red bow on and was in the parking lot at the apartment when she came home from school. She was overjoyed, and we were all so happy to be together. I'm not going to lie. This was not an easy time; the apartment had no washer or dryer, and I would have to hump laundry down 3 flights of outside steps and go to a laundromat to wash and dry and then hump the folded laundry up 3 flights of steps! Money was tight and there were times that my husband would be gone from 6:00 am until 11:00 pm because of the distance he was traveling selling construction jobs. I can remember the 1st Christmas we spent in the apartment being so minuscule that our Christmas tree had only 3 gifts under it for our daughter.

After April of 2015, when they closed my school, I didn't even have a cell phone. I was closed off from the world on the 3rd-floor apartment with no communication or money! I can recall my daughter and I eating Roman noodles for dinner that we purchased at the dollar store. On June 24th, 2015, Harry, Nadia, and I were at the Cherry Hill Mall picking up work boots for my husband when a huge storm hit! As we drove down Rt 55, tree branches were flying across the highway. My husband pulled over because it was unsafe to drive. Cars were aligned up and down the highway on both sides. We sat on the side of the highway for close to 30 minutes. When we made our way back to our apartment there were trees down everywhere, the town was dark, no electricity anywhere for miles! Sirens were going off, and it looked as if a tornado came through. When we got back to the apartment, it was dark, and after Nadia entered her bedroom, she began screaming, water is pouring on my bed! Sure enough, her bed was soaked, but more concerning was the huge tree that was through her ceiling and hanging in her room! My husband hung plastic on the ceiling around the tree to try and keep as much water out as possible. Nadia slept on the sofa. This storm was the worst I've ever seen in my lifetime. Roads were closed, trees were uprooted and blown over the roadways, electricity as well as SJ Gas was out, and electrical wires were dangling from poles and sparking! The world had stopped, and everything was closed, and the heat was unbearable!

I remember Harry and I trying to make our way to my mother's house to check on her, and every way we went, there were trees blocking our way. We finally made it to her house, and she was okay and had already begun gathering flashlights and candles so she could get through the night safely. No one knew at the time that we would be living like pioneers for over 2 weeks before the utilities would return. It was a lifestyle that I would not wish on my worst enemy.

In July of 2016, we would move out of the apartment to a rented home in Franklinville, NJ. This house was built in 1930, and my husband's cousin owned it. This transition was everything but easy. We had to empty our home out and bring the furniture to the house in Franklinville. My son, my husband, and his cousin were working on this old farmhouse for 6 weeks, trying to make it livable. Again, Murphy's Law bit me in the ass! We were out of the apartment but had no CO for the house, which meant we could not move in! We would have to wait until dark and sneak into the house to sleep and vacate it before dawn. My son Harry Jr. moved to San Francisco to stay with his sister, my youngest daughter, and I can recall days when the temperature reached 90+ degrees, and Nadia and I would walk through stores just to get cool while my husband worked. WaWa hot dogs were our lunch, and dinners were not much better. Fast food restaurants or WaWa hoagies were the best it got!

On August 10, 2016, we finally received a CO to move into the farmhouse. We would then begin to clean out our home in Sewell. Because the home had all utilities turned off, the pipes froze and broke, and there was a foot of water in our basement. All our treasures that were stored in the basement were lost! The house reeked from mold, and we had to wear masks to enter the house and pack up our clothes, dishes, furniture, lamps, paper-work, etc. We spent over two weeks packing his pickup truck and my FJ to the gills, making at least 10 trips back and forth. We had no money to afford a storage unit, so everything that was worth anything got stored in the dining room of the farmhouse; there were many things that we didn't get as time had run out, and the home no longer belonged to us! The biggest loss was an outside nativity that my Aunt Sis bought me from John Wanamaker's when they closed. I so loved Christmas, and that nativity was beautiful and irreplaceable. My husband still says today that if I didn't have so many shoes that filled his pick-up bed alone, we might have been able to get the Nativity Statues. I must admit, I was a shoe fanatic and had way too many shoes and boots. I also owned a lot of jewelry that most got sold for money to survive!

Senior Privilege

September arrived, and It was Nadia's senior year. Because she was a senior, she was allowed to continue her last year of HS at Clearview High School even though we were no longer residents in the district. The downfall was she had to get up at the crack of dawn to get ready and drive to Mullica Hill from Frank-linville, she needed to arrive by 7:15 AM to be on time for classes to begin. We lived about 18 miles away. It was a sacrifice, but she did it, and on June 17th, 2017, she received her diploma. This was a very proud moment for both my husband and myself. She would be our 5th child who graduated from Clearview Regional HS. This was the same HS I graduated from in 1978!

All was well until she was visiting with her boyfriend over in Sewell, and got in a car accident coming home at dusk. She was not hurt, but her car was totaled. She would be without a car until December of 2021 when Kristin (her sister) and Joe (brother-in-law) would give her a 1996 Toyota Camry that they owned after Joe bought a brand new Toyota Tundra. The Toyota Camry would be Nadia's. It was on Christmas Eve in 2001 that she would be given this gift; she was so grateful and cried like a baby! She still drives this car today!

In 2021, Nadia got a job at Friendly's as a server, hostess, and fountain girl making fabulous ice cream sundaes. She has become a very self-sufficient young lady in spite of dealing with a learning disability known as dyscalculia. This syndrome is similar to dyslexia, but with dyscalculia, it affects numbers and math concepts, so her reading skills are not affected, but her math skills are challenged. She has found ways to cope with this and is a very strong, competent young lady, and we are proud to be her parents.

The Loss of an Angel

In January 2019, I lost the Best Aunt in the world; she was not just an aunt but one of my best friends. She was always there for me, she worked at Kiddie Korral Kastle up until she was ill. She was kind to everyone and her spirit was so uplifting, filled with compassion and generosity. Anyone who knew her loved her. I will miss her more than words can explain. However, I knew on January 24, 2019, she received her Angel Wings and will be watching over me. Within a few days after she passed, I had a Cardinal visit that would actually peck on the sunroom window at exactly 9:00 am; this happened for 3 days straight! I know in my heart it was Aunt Sis saying goodbye. I'm certain the Heaven Gates opened wide for her entrance. I love you forever "Aunt Sis."

A Scary Time

In 2020, the world suffered the biggest Pandemic in my lifetime. Covid 19 caused world panic and many deaths. The schools were closed, businesses were shut down, and fear ruled the world! No one left their homes for months, and having compromised lungs, I became a shut-in. I really thought this was going to wipe out civilization. So many people lost their lives. Working at home on computers became standard. Children went to school on computers. Getting food to feed your family became a fight.

At the grocery stores, customers were required to line up outside, where their temperatures were checked, and they were provided with a paper mask covering their mouth and nose before being allowed to enter. Supplies were rationed, and even basic items like toilet paper became as valuable as gold! My husband was the brave one to shop for our groceries, and I was wiping everything down with disinfectant prior to bringing anything into our home. When they started giving out vaccines, we signed up to receive ours. This would prove to be a mistake for me; shortly after I received my second vaccine, I developed a blood clot in my leg and was put on blood thinners that I took for a year. No one knows for certain that the vaccines caused my blood clot, but because statistics show that many who received the vaccines developed blood clots, I'm never getting another Covid 19 vaccine!

During this Covid 19 time, my daughter and her family drove from San Francisco to NJ. She was moving back home, and although I feared them driving across the country and staying in motels along the way, I was overjoyed that she was moving back home! I would now be able to see my two beautiful granddaughters. The sad part would be that my daughter Erin would be alone in San Francisco. She had a good job as a Beer Sales Rep as well as a thriving Trivia Business. Kristin, who worked at home on her computer, gave her the opportunity to come home to New Jersey.

Epilogue

It is 2024, and it's almost 10 years since I've lost my school.

There have been good times and bad. There have been many tears over all my losses. In less than three months, I will be on Medicare and officially retired. I have suffered through many medical problems, such as a blood clot in my right leg, a retina bleed in my left eye, countless bouts of pneumonia as well as having Covid 19! My husband has suffered nerve damage in his cervical spine, which has caused him severe pain in his back and some loss of function in his left hand, which is a real problem because he is a lefty. Our son Harry has moved back from Pasadena, California, to NJ and is living with us. I would love to say that everything is wonderful and peachy keen, but that would be a lie, and if I am nothing else, I'm honest to a fault. I have made many mistakes throughout my life and have said or done things that I wish I could take back.

However, we all know you can never go back, only forward. I have learned many lessons, but I will tell you that the biggest lesson I have learned is to appreciate every day, no matter whether it's a good day or bad. Count your Blessings, not your problems, and appreciate what you have, even if it's not what you wished you had. There is always someone out there who wishes they had what you did. There is always room for improvement, and never give up on the opportunity to find it.

Do not dwell on things you cannot change; remember the serenity prayer. Cherish your loved ones and tell them you love them every chance you have. Remember to do something every day to brighten someone else's day. Remember the Golden Rule: treat others as you would want to be treated. Dwelling on regret only wastes precious time, so live with purpose and make each day meaningful.

Take time for yourself, whether it's reading a book or exercising, to recharge your mind and body. Embrace self-love and care for your well-being. Most importantly, seek guidance and support through prayer, asking God for help when you need it. It was God who made sure I entered this world; it was God who made sure I was placed with two loving parents when my birth mother couldn't keep me. It was God who blessed me with three biological children and directed me to Russia to adopt two children.

In fact, it was God who rode my bumper and kept me safe for 64 years. Although I have been cursed with this Murphy's Law I have been led by God to many serendipitous moments. There are too many coincidences in my life not to add up to the most important factor: I was truly blessed! I was meant to be here; God had a plan! So, the reason I felt compelled to write this book was to help others out there who may be sick, who may be financially struggling, or who may be lost.

You're not alone; my life has been rough. I've suffered from a disease from age 28 and was not diagnosed until my late thirties. I missed the best years of my life in hospitals. I lost everything in the end because of it. I have learned to be grateful for the little things and Thank God for my blessings. I may never find the truth as to why I was accused of doing things I did not do, but I thank God every night that he gave me the strength to write this book. There are many who will wonder why I would bare my soul and tell my story, and the answer is easy: why not?

Dedication for two special Mothers

To the Mother who raised me, "Mom," God couldn't have given me anyone more worthy. You have been my Best Mom as well as my Best Friend. You picked me up when I fell and celebrated my every success. You put all the band-aids on my boo-boos, and your love was always unconditional. I thank God for giving me you every day of my life! I love you "Always and Forever" Xoxo

To the Mother who gave me life. Without you, I would not be here! I thank you for the gift of life. I thank you for meeting me and accepting me as part of your family when my husband contacted you. I appreciate getting to know you and my sisters and brothers. Never regret the decision you made. I truly was blessed by the choice you made. Thank you. Xoxo